Welcome to the 1st edition of the *Handy Guide to British English: Understanding the "English" Language.* A few years ago I left the US to take a job in the UK and quickly found that, although we were all speaking English, there were many differences that often made it difficult for me to understand the British.

In fact, there were so many different words and phrases I heard at work and on TV (*telly*) that I started logging the words in my smart phone (*mobile*). Then I met my future wife in Manchester (*a Manc*), and from that day on we have laughed at my lack of understanding of the everyday words and phrases she was using. Before I knew it we had accumulated quite a list of British words and phrases, along with various British foods, that we thought could be of use to others.

This book was written based a comparison of British English to American English. We've included chapters on everyday words and phrases, differences in spelling and pronunciation, grammatical differences, and other handy information. Where there's no equivalent word or phrase in American

Introduction

English, we've indicated 'n/a' for 'not applicable', followed by a definition.

We have also included a handy chapter on British food, of which there are many differences to American cuisine. If you travel to the UK, be sure to enjoy the many different types of British food and drink. This chapter will be most helpful upon visiting any *pub* or restaurant in the UK.

If you travel to other parts of the world, you will find that British English and British cultural influence is far reaching. Chapter 5 contains a list of countries in the Commonwealth (former British Empire) where you will find signage and language using British English spelling and other influences.

Please note that we have also included a number of slang words and some with derogatory meanings that are not intended to offend, but simply intended to educate you in recognizing (*recognising*) insults and to avoid the misuse of related words. Knowing the meaning of some of the more common insults or derogatory phrases that you may hear in everyday conversation could save you from some awkward moments. For example, if you hear a Brit talk about

Introduction

shagging, they're not talking about dancing to beach music! This book can save you from some embarrassing mistakes.

We have compiled this handy guide in hopes that it will be both informative and fun for anyone visiting any area of the United Kingdom or while watching British TV shows or movies (*films*), and/or when reading British novels. We hope you find it both fun and informative.

Cheers!

Mike and Nina

Acknowledgements

First and foremost, I thank God for the ability to write this handy guide and for the opportunity to live and work abroad and travel around His incredible creation.

I would like to thank Nina, my lovely wife whom I met in Manchester, and her children Danielle and Luke, who have frequently *taken the Mickey out of me* over the last few years at my lack of understanding of their version of the English language. Thank you Nina, for your numerous contributions to the content contained herein and your patience while putting it all together.

I would also like to thank Geoff L., who *collected* me from the airport on my very first day in the UK, helped me get *sorted*, and began enlightening me on the English way. Many thanks *mate!*

Finally, I dedicate this book to my wonderful adult children, Kendall and Kayla, who are my inspiration for life.

Mike Danford

Table of Contents

Introduction   1

Acknowledgements   4

Chapter 1 – Everyday Words & Phrases (A to Zed)   6

Chapter 2 – British Food   95

Chapter 3 – Grammatical Differences   112

Chapter 4 – Pronunciation and Spelling   122

Chapter 5 – Other Handy Information   139

Chapter 6 – Sources   152

Handy Guide to British English:
Understanding the "English" Language

Chapter 1 – Everyday Words and Phrases (A to Zed)

A

UK says:	USA says:
AA (acronym for Automotive Association)	Roadside assistance (similar to 'Triple A' in the US)
A&E (acronym for Accidents and Emergency at UK hospitals)	ER, Emergency Room
Absobloodylutely	Yes! Absolutely! (with emphasis)
ABTA	n/a; Association of British Travel Agents
Accelerator pedal	Gas pedal
Accumulator	Rechargeable battery
Ace	Excellent, right on
Across the patch	Across the entire… (can refer to an entire organization or locale)
Action man	Macho man
Action replay	Instant replay
Advert	Commercial, advertisement
Advocate (Scotland)	Attorney (see also 'barrister')
Aerial	Antenna
Aerofoil	Airfoil
Aeroplane	Airplane (see Chapter 4 – Pronunciation and Spelling)

Chapter 1 - Everyday Words and Phrases (A to Zed)

UK says:	USA says:
Air biscuit	Fart
Airy fairy	Wussy, weakling
Afters	Dessert (after the entrée)
Agony aunt	Advice columnist
Aggro	Aggravated
Alba	n/a; the Gaelic name for Scotland
Aled up	Drunk
Alight	Get off, disembark a mode of transportation such as a plane or train
All mouth and no trousers	Cocky or hollow boasting
All over the shop	Disorganized
All piss and wind	All talk and no action
All to pot	Gone to pot, something gone wrong
Allen key	Allen wrench
Aluminium	Aluminum (see Chapter 4 - Pronunciation and Spelling)
Amber	Yellow (amber is typically used in UK instead of yellow as in 'red, amber, green' in traffic lights)
Anchors	Brakes (on a car)

Chapter 1 – Everyday Words and Phrases (A to Zed)

UK says:	USA says:
Ankle biters	Children (derogatory term)
Anorak	Raincoat; light waterproof jacket
Antenatal	Prenatal
Anti-clockwise	Counter-clockwise
Any road	Anyway
Argy bargy	Disagreement, argument
Arrows	Darts (describes the actual darts used in the game of darts)
Arse	Buttocks; milder form of ass
Arse about face	Back to front
Arsemonger	Contemptuous person
Arse over elbow	Head over heels
Arse over tit	Head over heels (derogatory)
As well	Also, too ("I will have another ale, as well"); Brits usually don't say 'also' or 'too'
Asymmetric bars	Uneven bars (gymnastics)
Athletics	Track and field
Aubergine	Eggplant
Autocue	Teleprompter

Handy Guide to British English: Understanding the "English" Language

Chapter 1 – Everyday Words and Phrases (A to Zed)

UK says:	USA says:
Autumn	Fall (Brits do not use 'fall' for the season that precedes winter)
Aye (pronounced 'I')	Yes
Axe	Guitar
Axe wound	Vagina

Chapter 1 – Everyday Words and Phrases (A to Zed)

B

UK says:	USA says:
Babby	Baby
Baby batter	Semen
Baccy or backy	Tobacco
Backhander	Bribe
Baffies (Scotland)	Slippers
Bagsies	Dibs (as in calling dibs on going first, riding shotgun, etc.)
Bairn (Scotland)	Child
Bairnskip (Scotland)	Childhood
Bait	Homemade lunch taken to work
Ball bag	Scrotum
Bang on	Correct
Bang out of order	Totally unacceptable
Bang to rights	Caught in the act
Bangers	see Chapter 2 – British Food
Bank holiday	Public holiday; government or legal holiday
Banque (used less frequently today)	Bank
Baking tray	Cookie sheet
Bap	see Chapter 2 – British Food

Chapter 1 – Everyday Words and Phrases (A to Zed)

UK says:	USA says:
Bargepole (I wouldn't touch that with a bargepole)	Ten-foot pole (I wouldn't touch that with a ten-foot pole)
Barrister	Lawyer, attorney (high court litigator)
Barber's shop	Barbershop
Barking	Crazy, insane (see also 'mad')
Barm	see Chapter 2 – British Food
Barmy	Foolish, silly, strange
Barmy army	n/a; group of overly zealous fans in support of a specific sports team
Bat (as in table tennis)	Paddle
Bawbees (Scotland)	Money
Bawd (Scotland)	Rabbit
Beaker	Sippy cup
Beans on toast	see Chapter 2 – British Food
Beastly	Nasty or unpleasant person
Beeb or The Beeb	n/a; BBC (British Broadcasting Corporation)
Bee's knees	Outstanding; excellent
Beetroot	Beets
Bell, as in 'give me a bell'	Call, give me a call
Bell-end	Idiot, dickhead (literally the head of a penis)
Belt up	Shut up
Ben (Scotland)	Mountain

Handy Guide to British English: Understanding the "English" Language

Chapter 1 - Everyday Words and Phrases (A to Zed)

UK says:	USA says:
Bender	Gay man; a wild drinking spree
Bent as a nine bob note	Corrupt, very dishonest
Berk	Stupid idiot
Bespoke	Custom made
Best of British	Good luck (expression)
Bickey	see Chapter 2 - British Food
Big dog	Big man
Biggie	Poo, poop, do-do, dookey (what a UK child calls poo)
Bill (at restaurant)	Check
Billie (Scotland)	Brother, companion
Bin	Trash can
Bin it	Throw it away
Bingo wings	n/a; refers to the flabby skin under an unfit woman's arm
Bird	Woman (usually attractive)
Biro	Ball-point pen
Biscuits	see Chapter 2 - British Food
Bite your arm off	Overly excited
Bits and bobs	Odds and ends
Blag	Wing it
Black pudding	see Chapter 2 - British Food

Chapter 1 – Everyday Words and Phrases (A to Zed)

UK says:	USA says:
Bladdered	Drunk, wasted
Blanket bath	Sponge bath
Bleeper	Pager, beeper
Blimey	Oh no! or Oh my gosh! (derived from saying 'God blind me')
Blinkered	Narrow minded
Bloater	see Chapter 2 – British Food
Block of flats	Apartment building
Bloke	Man, guy
Bloody	n/a; probably the Brits' favorite adjective to express anger, frustration, or just for emphasis; similar to damn
Bloody Hell	Damn!; similar to "You gotta be kidding me!"
Blow off	Fart
Blow your own trumpet	Toot your own horn, brag
Blower	Telephone (land line)
Blues and twos	Emergency vehicle (with lights and siren)
Bob	Money

Chapter 1 – Everyday Words and Phrases (A to Zed)

UK says:	USA says:
Bobbie	Cop, policeman
Bob's your uncle	Everything is alright and that's it (expression), there ya go, that's it
Bodge	Jerry-rigged, something done quick and dirty
Boffin	Expert
Bog	Toilet
Bog roll	Toilet paper
Bogey	Booger (as in picking your nose)
Boiler suit	Coveralls
Bollocks	Balls (as in men's testicles); also can mean rubbish or crap
Bomb	Success, something that goes strikingly well ("I bombed my maths quiz")
Bombing it	Traveling at high speeding
Bonfire Night	November 5th fireworks and bonfire commemoration of the failed Gunpowder Plot of 1605
Bonk	Sex

Chapter 1 – Everyday Words and Phrases (A to Zed)

UK says:	USA says:
Bonking	Having sex
Bon mot	Witty remark
Bonnet (of a car)	Hood
Bonnie	Pretty
Boob	Mistake
Boob tube	Tube top (women's tube top); in the UK 'boob tube' is not associated with TV
Book (as in to book a room)	Reserve, make a reservation
Boot (of a car)	Trunk
Boggin (Scottish)	Smelly, dirty
Bottle	Courage, no fear (often associated with drinking, 'liquid courage')
Bottom drawer	Hope chest
Boxing Day	Day after Christmas
Boys in blue	Policemen
Blootered (Scotland)	Drunk, wasted
Braces	Suspenders
Brackets ( )	Parentheses
Brass	Money
Brassed off	Angry, pissed off
Brass monkeys	Freezing cold outside
Break (in school)	Recess
Breakdown van	Tow truck
Breeks (Scottish)	Pants, see 'trousers'
Breeze block	Cinder block

Handy Guide to British English: Understanding the "English" Language

Chapter 1 - Everyday Words and Phrases (A to Zed)

UK says:	USA says:
Brekky	Breakfast
Brew	Cup of tea
Brilliant, Brill	Awesome, excellent (short for brilliant)
Bristol fashion	Ship shape, neat and orderly
Brolly	Umbrella
Brown sauce	see Chapter 2 – British Food
Budge up	Move over, make room
Budgie / budgerigar	Parakeet
Buffet	n/a; the refreshments cart on a passenger train
Bugger	Jerk
Bugger all	Something cheap or free; nothing
Buggered	Broken ("My laptop is buggered")
Buggery	Anal sex
Bulkhead	Firewall
Bum	Butt, buttocks
Bum bag	Fanny pack
Bumf	Useless paperwork
Bung	Throw or toss; can also reference a bribe
Bungalow	Ranch-style house

Chapter 1 – Everyday Words and Phrases (A to Zed)

UK says:	USA says:
Bunk off	Play hooky or call in sick; skirt assigned duties
Bureau	Writing table
Burgle	Burglarize, break into a building
Burn (Scotland)	Creek or narrow stream
Busker	Street performer
Busking	Performing in the street for money
Butchers	To have a look at something
Butchery	Slaughterhouse
Butty	see Chapter 2 – British Food

Chapter 1 – Everyday Words and Phrases (A to Zed)

C

UK says:	USA says:
C of E	n/a; Church of England
Caff	Café
Call box	Phone booth
Cake	see Chapter 2 – British Food
Cake hole	Pie hole; mouth (as in "Shut your cake hole")
Camp	Gay or gayish, effeminate behavior
Camp bed	Cot placed inside a tent
Campsite	Campground
Candy floss	Cotton candy
Cannie (Scotland)	Smart (a cannie lad)
Capsicum	Bell peppers
Car journey	Road trip
Car park	Parking lot
Car valeting	Auto detailing
Caravan	RV (recreation vehicle)
Cardie	Short for cardigan (sweater)
Caretaker	Custodian (of a building)
Carrier bag	Shopping bag
Carry on	Continue

Chapter 1 – Everyday Words and Phrases (A to Zed)

UK says:	USA says:
Carvery	n/a; restaurant or pub that serves freshly cooked meal with cut meat and sides at a fixed price
Cash machine	ATM
Cash point	ATM
Casket	Jewelry box
Catapult	Slingshot
Cats eyes	Reflectors (on a highway that resemble small eyes)
Caught the sun	Got a tan
Chancer	Risk taker
Chankin (Scotland)	Cold, very cold
Chap	Man or boy
Chat up	Pick up (as 'chat up' a girl in a pub)
Chav or chavvy	Low class similar to 'trailer trash'
Checker	Inspector
Cheeky	Overly clever or a bit risqué
Cheerio	Goodbye
Cheers	Hello or goodbye or thanks; also a drinking toast
Cheesed off	Upset, pissed
Chemist	Pharmacist
Cheque	Check; see Chapter 3 – Pronunciation and Spelling

Chapter 1 – Everyday Words and Phrases (A to Zed)

UK says:	USA says:
Chew	Taffy
Child minder	Baby sitter
Chimney pot	Chimney cap; top of a rooftop smoke stack
Chin wag	Chit chat
Chip in	Chime in
Chippy/chippie	Fish and chips shop
Chips	French fries
Chivvy	Hurry
Chock-a-block	Tight or closely packed as in a schedule
Chocka	Overly crowded as in traffic or shopping center
Chocolate drops	Chocolate chips
Christmas bauble	Christmas ornament
Christmas cracker	Traditional Christmas dinner gift; tube with a small explosive pop when opened containing a small prize, a joke, and paper crown
Chuffed	Pleased, stoked
Chuffer	All talk and no action
Chunder	Vomit
Cider	see Chapter 2 – British Food
Ciggy	Cigarette
Cinderella	n/a; used in sports for an underachieving team

Handy Guide to British English:
Understanding the "English" Language

Chapter 1 – Everyday Words and Phrases (A to Zed)

UK says:	USA says:
Cinema	Movie theater, the movies
City centre	Downtown
Clanger	Big mistake (as in to 'lay an egg')
Clapped out	Worn out
Clear off	Get lost
Cleg	Horse fly
Cling film	Plastic wrap
Cloakroom	Bathroom, public restroom
Close	Cul-de-sac
Clothes peg	Clothes pin
Clotted cream	see Chapter 2 – British Food
Coach	Bus
Cobblers	Nonsense, see 'rubbish'
Cocked it up	Messed up, screwed up
Cockney	n/a; generally someone from East London
Codswallop	Load of crap, baloney
Collect	Pick up ("Joe collected me from the metro stop")
College	Not the same as US; in the UK it is the level of education between primary school and university (akin to high school)

Chapter 1 – Everyday Words and Phrases (A to Zed)

UK says:	USA says:
Collywobbles	Upset or nervous stomach; see also 'dicky stomach'
Colour	Color; see Chapter 4 – Pronunciation and Spelling
Come round	Come over
Come round to mine	Come over to my house
Comet	see Chapter 2 – British Food
Compo	Compensation
Compulsory purchase	Eminent domain (govt. power to take private property for public use)
Concession	Discount (usually to a specific group like senior citizens or students)
Conk	Nose
Conkers	Chestnuts
Constabulary	Police
Cooker	Oven
Copper	Policeman
Coriander	Cilantro (the herb)
Corking	Excellent, outstanding
Corn	Wheat (England); oats (Scotland)
Coshing	Bludgeoning
Costermonger	n/a; seller of fruit and vegetables
Cot	Crib

Chapter 1 – Everyday Words and Phrases (A to Zed)

UK says:	USA says:
Cot death	Crib death (SIDS)
Cotton bud; ear bud	Cotton swab, Q tip
Cotton wool	Cotton ball
Council houses	Housing project (government housing); "the projects"
Counterfoil	Check stub
Courgette	Zucchini
Course	Degree (the entire degree program)
Court shoes	High heels, pumps
Cow	Bitch, rude or contemptuous woman
Cozzy (short for costume, see 'swimming costume')	Bathing suit
Crack (as in 'to have a crack with')	Chat, conversation; also to have a laugh with
Crack on	Get going or continue on
Crackers	Nuts, crazy, insane
Cracking	Excellent ("We had a cracking view from our hotel room")
Crash barrier	Guard rail
Crèche	Day care or nursery school
Cream crackered	Bushed; exhausted
Crikey	n/a; an expression of surprise

Chapter 1 – Everyday Words and Phrases (A to Zed)

UK says:	USA says:
Crisps	Potato chips (see Chapter 2 – British Food)
Crossroads	Intersection
Crumpet	An attractive female (slang)
Crusty dragon	Booger (of the nose)
Cubicle	Stall (in a bathroom)
Culottes	Skorts (women's skirt-shorts combination)
Cuppa	Cup of tea
Current account	Checking account
Cutlery	Silverware
CV (curriculum vitae)	Resume

Chapter 1 – Everyday Words and Phrases (A to Zed)

D

UK says:	USA says:
Dabs	Fingerprints
Daft	Silly or foolish
Daft cow	Large, dumb woman (derogatory)
Damper (on a car)	Shock absorber
Danger money	Hazard pay
Dapper	Well dressed; sharp
Daps	Gym shoes, sneakers
Darbies	Handcuffs
Dead	n/a; a favorite adverb used for emphasis as in "That was dead easy" or "I'll be dead honest with you"
Dead beat	Exhausted; not to be confused with American 'deadbeat' (slacker)
Dead from the neck up	Very stupid
Dear	Expensive
Dekko	Have a look at something
De-mister (in dash of a car)	Defroster
De-plane	Exit an airplane
Destroyed	Drunk, intoxicated, high
Dialling tone	Dial tone
Diary	Calendar (as in a personal calendar or schedule)

Handy Guide to British English:
Understanding the "English" Language

Chapter 1 – Everyday Words and Phrases (A to Zed)

UK says:	USA says:
DIC ('drunk in charge' of a motor vehicle)	DUI, DWI
Dicky stomach	Upset stomach
Diddle	Con, swindle, rip off
Digestives	see Chapter 2 – British Food
Dim	Stupid
Dinner jacket	Tuxedo
Dip	Pickpocket
Dip switch (in a car)	Dimmer switch (headlights)
Dishy	Attractive, good looking
Diversion	Detour
Do	Party (see also 'stag do')
Docker	Longshoreman
Doddle	Easy
Dodgems	Bumper cars
Dodgy	Shady, shifty, iffy, risky
Dog's bollocks	Looking good
Dog's dinner	Dapper, sharp dressed
Dogging	n/a; sex in a public place
Dole (as in 'on the dole')	Welfare benefits
Doll's house	Dollhouse
Done over	Beaten up
Doolally	n/a; expression of losing one's mind (from boredom)
Donder (Scotland)	A long walk
Donkey's years	Ages (as in "I haven't seen you in donkey's years")

Handy Guide to British English: Understanding the "English" Language

Chapter 1 – Everyday Words and Phrases (A to Zed)

UK says:	USA says:
Doofer	Thingamajig (unnamed object)
Dormitory town	Bedroom community
Doss	Lazy
Draper	Drapery dealer (dry goods)
Draining board	Drain board
Draughts (game)	Checkers
Drawing pins	Thumb tacks
Drawing room	Living room
Dressing gown	Bath robe
Drink driving	Drunk driving
Drinks cupboard	Liquor cabinet
Drinks party	Cocktail party
Driveaxle	Driveshaft
Driving licence	Driver's license
Drop a clanger	Make a gaffe, stick your foot in your mouth, faux-pas
Dual carriageway	Divided highway
Duck	Cricket term similar to strikeout in baseball (zero score for batsman); also used as a term of endearment similar to 'love'
Duff	Poor quality or non-functional, useless
Duffer	Useless (in reference to a person)

Handy Guide to British English: Understanding the "English" Language

Chapter 1 – Everyday Words and Phrases (A to Zed)

UK says:	USA says:
Dull as a dishwasher	Extremely boring
Dummy	Pacifier
Dunderhead (Scotland)	An idiot or tool
Dust sheet	Drop cloth
Dustbin	Garbage can
Dustman	Garbage man
Duvet	Bed comforter
Dux	Valedictorian
Dynamo	Electric generator

Chapter 1 - Everyday Words and Phrases (A to Zed)

E

UK says:	USA says:
Ear-bashing	An ear full, severe reprimand
Earner	n/a; a job that pays well
Earwig	Eavesdrop
Easy peasy	Very easy
Earth (electrical)	Ground
Eating irons	Silverware
Electric fire	Space heater
Electrics	n/a; electrical fittings in a house
Elevenses	n/a; a mid-morning snack
Elk	Moose
End away	Sex (to have sex)
Engaged	Busy, in use, occupied ("The toilet is engaged")
Engineer	Technician who repairs and operates machinery
Ensuite (on suite)	Bathroom connected to bedroom (i.e. master bath)

Handy Guide to British English:
Understanding the "English" Language

Chapter 1 – Everyday Words and Phrases (A to Zed)

UK says:	USA says:
Estate agent	Realtor, real estate agent
Envisage	Envision
Essex girl	n/a; derogatory stereotype for a loose and ditzy girl (similar to 'dumb blond')
Estate car	Station wagon
Ex-directory	Unlisted (as in phone number)
Expiry	Expiration

Chapter 1 – Everyday Words and Phrases (A to Zed)

F

UK says:	USA says:
Facia (of a car)	Dashboard
Fag	Cigarette
Fag end	Cigarette butt
Fagged	Bothered, interrupted
Faggot	Meatball of seasoned liver
Fair (hair)	Blonde
Fairy cake	Cupcake
Fairy lights	Christmas lights
Fancy (as in "I fancy her")	Attracted to
Fancy a...? (as in "fancy an ale?")	Would you like a...?
Fancy dress	Costume
Fancy dress party	Costume party
Fancy woman	Mistress; woman on the side
Fanny	Vagina
Fanny Adams (Sweet Fanny Adams)	Nothing at all; euphemism for 'f*ck all'
Fanny around, fanny about	Procrastinate
Father Christmas	Santa Claus
Fault finding	Troubleshooting
Feart (Scotland)	Scared
Fell	Small mountain
Fell walking	Mountain hiking
Fete	Outdoor charity bazaar
Filch	Steal or pilfer

Chapter 1 – Everyday Words and Phrases (A to Zed)

UK says:	USA says:
Filing cabinet	File cabinet
Film	Movie
Fire engine	Fire truck
First floor	Second floor (UK starts with ground floor)
Fiscal year	Financial year
Fish fingers	Fish sticks
Fishmonger	n/a; person or shop that sells fish
Fit	Sexy, someone who is attractive, hot
Fiver	n/a; 5 pound British note (five quid)
Fix	Arrange or set (a date)
Fizzy drink	Soda or pop (carbonated drink), soft drink
Flannel	Wash cloth
Flat	Apartment
Flatmate	Roommate
Flat tyre	Flat tire
Flexitime	Flextime

Chapter 1 – Everyday Words and Phrases (A to Zed)

UK says:	USA says:
Flick knife	Switchblade
Flog	n/a; to sell something that is not worth the price
Flogging a dead horse	Beating a dead horse
Fluff	Dryer lint
Flutter	Place a bet
Fly tipping	Littering
Flyover	Overpass
Food shopping	Grocery shopping
Football	Soccer
Football boots	Cleats
Football pitch	Soccer field
Foot path	Hiking trail
Fortnightly	Every 2 weeks
Freehold	n/a; real estate ownership of both the land and building; see also 'Leasehold'
Freephone	Toll-free number
Freewheeling	Coasting (as in car)
French letter	Condom
Fringe (as in hair style)	Bangs

Handy Guide to British English: Understanding the "English" Language

Chapter 1 - Everyday Words and Phrases (A to Zed)

UK says:	USA says:
Frog	French person (derogatory slang)
Full board	All-inclusive
Full of beans	Full of energy
Full stop (as in punctuation)	Period
Fun fair	Carnival, fair

Chapter 1 – Everyday Words and Phrases (A to Zed)

G

UK says:	USA says:
G clamp	C clamp
Gaff	Home
Gaffer tape	Duct tape
Gagging	Desperate for (usually derogatory in reference to a woman gagging for sex)
Gammon	Ham
Gammy	Injured, lame
Gander	Have a look at something
Gannet	Greedy person
Garage	Auto repair shop
Garden	Yard; lawn
GBP	n/a; Great Britain Pound (international currency indicator; similar to USD)
Gear lever	Gear shift
Gearbox	Transmission (of an car)
Gearing (as in finances)	Leveraging
Gear-level	Gearshift
Geezer	Gangster
Geggy (Scotland)	Mouth
Gen	Information
Geordie	n/a; generally someone from northeast England
Get	see 'git'

Chapter 1 – Everyday Words and Phrases (A to Zed)

UK says:	USA says:
Get on	n/a; to do something
Get stuffed!	Go screw yourself!
Get the hump	Get annoyed with
Gherkin	Pickle
Giddy	Vertigo
Giddy kipper	Overly excited
Gilet	n/a; padded outdoor vest
Ginger	Red head
Ginger beer	Homosexual, fruit
Girl Guide	Girl Scout
Git	Annoying, stupid, childish, incompetent person; moron
Give way (traffic)	Yield
Glandular fever	Mononucleosis (mono)
Gob	Mouth
Gobby	Opinionated, offensive, loud and obnoxious
Gobshite	Bullsh*t
Gobsmacked	Flabbergasted, speechless, amazed, blown away
Gogglebox	Television
Golf buggy	Golf cart
Gone off	Spoiled or expired (as in the milk has gone off)
Goods train	Freight train
Goolies	Balls, nuts, testicles

Chapter 1 – Everyday Words and Phrases (A to Zed)

UK says:	USA says:
Gooseberry	Third wheel in a relationship that affects their courting
Gormless	Foolish, clueless
Governor	Boss
GP (General Practitioner)	General Physician
Graft	Hard work
Grammar school	Elementary school
Grass	Snitch, informant
Green finger	Green thumb
Griller	Broiler
Grockle	Tourist (derogatory)
Grotty	Disgusting, dirty
Ground floor	First floor
Groundsman	Groundskeeper
Grub	Food (see 'pub grub')
Guard (railways)	Conductor
Guff	Nonsense, silly talk
Gum (adhesive)	Glue
Gum shield	Mouth guard (sports)
Gutted	Highly disappointed
Gutties (Scotland)	Shoes

Chapter 1 – Everyday Words and Phrases (A to Zed)

H

UK says:	USA says:
Hacked off	Ticked off, peeved
Haich (pronunciation for the letter 'H')	H
Hair slide	Barrette
Half board	n/a; meal plan where only breakfast and lunch are covered
Half cast	Mixed race
Half nine (for telling time); half [any hour 1 – 12]	9:30; 30 minutes after the hour
Handbag	Purse (woman's)
Handbrake (in a car)	Emergency brake
Hand luggage	Carry on (luggage)
Hank marvin	Starving; very hungry
Hard cheese	Bad luck
Hard lines	Bad luck
Hard shoulder	n/a; paved shoulder on side of a highway
Hash symbol (#)	Pound sign (#)
Hat stand	Hat rack
Have a go	Give it a try
Havering (Scotland)	Talking silly, nonsense
Having kittens	Extremely nervous
Headmaster (as in school)	Principal
Health and Safety (H&S)	Safety rules and regulations

Chapter 1 – Everyday Words and Phrases (A to Zed)

UK says:	USA says:
Heaving	Extremely crowded
Heckers like	n/a; something didn't happen, 'like hell it is!'
Hen do	Bachelorette party
Her Majesty's pleasure	Put in jail
Higgledy piggledy	Jumbled up, disarray
High street	Main street
Hire	Rent
Hire car	Rental car
Hire purchase	Installment plan
Hiya	Hello, hi
HMRC	n/a; acronym for Her Majesty's Revenue & Customs (similar to the IRS)
HMS	n/a; acronym for Her Majesty's Ship, the prefix for all Royal Navy vessels
Hob	Stove top
Hockey	Field hockey (not ice hockey)
Holdall	Carryall
Hold to account	Hold accountable
Holiday (on holiday)	Vacation (on vacation)
Holidaymaker	Vacationer
Home from home	Home away from home
Home run	Home stretch (has nothing to do with baseball)

Chapter 1 – Everyday Words and Phrases (A to Zed)

UK says:	USA says:
Homely	Homey
Honking	Being sick, throwing up
Hood (of a car)	Convertible top (the folding fabric top)
Hoodie	Hooded sweatshirt
Hoo-ha	Argument
Hooker	Position in rugby football
Hooter	Steam whistle or siren of a factory that indicates the start/stop of a workday; also can refer to the nose
Hoovering	Vacuuming
Horses for courses	To each his own
Hot flush	Hot flash
Housepipe	Garden hose
How did you find it?	How did you like it? (has nothing to do with location)
How the land lies	What the situation is
How's your father?	Sexual intercourse (euphemism)
Hum	Foul smell
Hump	Depression (She's in a hump)

Chapter 1 – Everyday Words and Phrases (A to Zed)

I

UK says:	USA says:
I'm easy	I don't care, it's all the same to me
I'm off to Bedfordshire	I'm off to bed, hitting the hay
Ice lolly	Ice pop
Icing sugar	Confectionary or powdered sugar
Ickle	Tiny; something very small
Identity parade	Police lineup
Indicator (for a car)	Turn signal
Inside leg	Inseam
Interior light (of a car)	Dome light
Intern	Replacement
Interval	Intermission (as in a play)
Invigilator	Proctor (of a test or exam)
Ironmonger	Hardware store
Ivories	Teeth

Chapter 1 – Everyday Words and Phrases (A to Zed)

J

UK says:	USA says:
Jabs	Shots, vaccination
Jacket potato	Baked potato
Jaked (Scotland)	Drunk
Jam	Jelly
Jam sandwich	Police car
Jammy	Lucky
Jammy dodger	Lucky duck (someone with good luck)
Jelly	Gelatin dessert (jello)
Jelly babies	Jelly beans
Jerry	n/a; slang for someone from Germany
Jessie (Scottish)	Wimp, wussy
Jif	Idiot
Jim-jams	Pajamas, PJs
Jobby jabber (Scotland)	A gay man
Jobsworth	n/a; a meticulous rule-follower
Jock	A Scotsman (slang)
Joe Bloggs	Average Joe
Joe Public	John Q. Public
John Thomas	Penis

Chapter 1 – Everyday Words and Phrases (A to Zed)

UK says:	USA says:
Joinery	Carpentry
Joint	Piece of cooked meat for carving
Jolly	Very good
Jollies	Thrills
Josser	Simpleton
Joy	Satisfaction (as in accomplishing a task)
Jubblies	Boobs (slang for women's breasts)
Jug	Pitcher
Juggernaut	18-wheeler
Jumble sale	Rummage sale; garage sale
Jump	Have sex
Jump leads	Jumper cables
Jumped up	Arrogant, uppity

Chapter 1 – Everyday Words and Phrases (A to Zed)

UK says:	USA says:
Jumper	Sweater
Junior school	Elementary school
Just	Barely (We only just escaped)

Chapter 1 – Everyday Words and Phrases (A to Zed)

K

UK says:	USA says:
Kecks	Trousers
Keen	Eager, interested in
Keep Calm and Carry On	see Chapter 5 – Other Handy Information
Keeper	Goalie
Kerb	Curb
Kerfuffle	Scuffle or argument
Khazi	Toilet, bathroom
Kick off	Get angry
Kip	Nap
Kippers	See Chapter 2 – British Foods
Kirby grip	Bobby pin
Kit	Sports clothing or uniform; gear
Kitchen roll	Paper towels
Kiwi	New Zealander
Klaxon	n/a; emergency or warning alarm or siren, usually the 'ah-ooga' sound
Knackered	Tired; exhausted
Knackers	Testicles, balls

Handy Guide to British English: Understanding the "English" Language

Chapter 1 – Everyday Words and Phrases (A to Zed)

UK says:	USA says:
Knees up	A lively party
Knickers	Panties (women's underwear)
Knob	Penis
Knob head	Dick head (derogatory)
Knob jockey	Homosexual male
Knock on effect	Domino effect, repercussion, unintentional effect
Knock about	Rough play (in sports)
Knock up	Bang on a door, wake someone up (no reference to pregnancy)
Knocking shop	Brothel
Know your onions	Knowledgeable; know your stuff

Chapter 1 – Everyday Words and Phrases (A to Zed)

K

UK says:	USA says:
Kecks	Trousers
Keen	Eager, interested in
Keep Calm and Carry On	see Chapter 5 – Other Handy Information
Keeper	Goalie
Kerb	Curb
Kerfuffle	Scuffle or argument
Khazi	Toilet, bathroom
Kick off	Get angry
Kip	Nap
Kippers	See Chapter 2 – British Foods
Kirby grip	Bobby pin
Kit	Sports clothing or uniform; gear
Kitchen roll	Paper towels
Kiwi	New Zealander
Klaxon	n/a; emergency or warning alarm or siren, usually the 'ah-ooga' sound
Knackered	Tired; exhausted
Knackers	Testicles, balls

Handy Guide to British English: Understanding the "English" Language

Chapter 1 – Everyday Words and Phrases (A to Zed)

UK says:	USA says:
Knees up	A lively party
Knickers	Panties (women's underwear)
Knob	Penis
Knob head	Dick head (derogatory)
Knob jockey	Homosexual male
Knock on effect	Domino effect, repercussion, unintentional effect
Knock about	Rough play (in sports)
Knock up	Bang on a door, wake someone up (no reference to pregnancy)
Knocking shop	Brothel
Know your onions	Knowledgeable; know your stuff

Chapter 1 – Everyday Words and Phrases (A to Zed)

L

UK says:	USA says:
L-plate	n/a; special license plate required for Learners
Lad	Boy
Laddette	Boisterous woman who drinks alcohol
Ladybird	Ladybug
Lag	Inmate, convict
Lager	Beer
Lager lout	Drunk (with bad behavior)
Larder	Pantry
Lass	Girl
Latches	Locks
Laughing gear	Mouth
Launderette	Laundromat
Lay by	Rest area (on highways)
Lav	Toilet
Lead (pronounced 'leed')	Electrical cord; a leash
Learnt	Learned
Leasehold	n/a; possession rights to dwell without ownership (usually for 99 years)
Leave it to me	I'll take care of it
Lecky (Scotland)	Electric bill
Leg it	Hurry up; run hurriedly

Handy Guide to British English: Understanding the "English" Language

Chapter 1 – Everyday Words and Phrases (A to Zed)

UK says:	USA says:
Leg-over	Sex, a lay (an occurrence, as in 'She met a guy last night and got her leg-over')
Legless	Drunk, hammered
Lemonade	Carbonated citrus drink similar to 7-Up
Lessons	Classes
Let	Rent
Licence	License
Lie in	Sleep in (sleeping late into the morning)
Lie of the land	Lay of the land
Ligger	Moocher, freeloader
Lighted	Lit
Life assurance	Life insurance
Life preserver (weapon)	Blackjack
Lift	Elevator
Lilo	Pool float, pool inflatable
Limey	English person
Linn (Scottish)	Waterfall
Liquid lunch	Meal that consists of drinking alcohol more than eating the food
Lodger	Renter, tenant

Chapter 1 – Everyday Words and Phrases (A to Zed)

UK says:	USA says:
Loft	Attic
Lolly	Popsicle; also slang for money
Lollypop lady	Crossing guard
Loo	Bathroom
Look after	Take care of
Look smart	Be quick
Lorry	Big rig; tractor-trailer
Lost the plot	Gone mad
Lot (as in "That lot are making too much noise")	Group or bunch
Loudhailer	Megaphone, bullhorn
Lounge	Living room
Love (polite form of address, as in "Can I get you anything, Love?")	Honey or Sugar; similar to US Southerners as in "Can I get you anything, Honey?"
Love bites	Hickies
Low loader	Flatbed truck
Lucky dip	Grab bag
Luggage van (of a train)	Baggage car
Lurgy	Bug (illness); slang for a contagious but not severe unspecified illness

Handy Guide to British English: Understanding the "English" Language

Chapter 1 - Everyday Words and Phrases (A to Zed)

M

UK says:	USA says:
Mac (short for mackintosh)	Rain coat (full length raincoat)
Mad	Crazy, insane (typically used as "Are you mad?")
Maiden	Clothes dryer rack
Main	Line; pipe that carries gas or water
Main road	Highway
Mains power	Household electricity
Malkied (Scotland)	Drunk
Maize	Corn
Man flu	A severe head cold or upper respiratory infection
Managing Director (MD)	Chief Executive Officer (CEO)
Manc (short for Mancunian)	n/a; slang for someone from Manchester, UK
Mangetout	Snow peas
Manky	Filthy, dirty, disgusting
Mardy	Whiney, crybaby
Marks (as in school)	Grades
Marmalade	Jam; jelly
Marrow	Squash (vegetable)
Mashed	High, stoned
Mate	Buddy, pal, chum

Chapter 1 – Everyday Words and Phrases (A to Zed)

UK says:	USA says:
Maths	Mathematics
Meat and two veg	Male genitalia
Mental	Crazy or insane
Mentioned in despatches	Decorated (for valor or gallantry)
Mews	Alley
Miffed	Peeved; pissed off
Mile-ometer	Speedometer
Milk run	Safe patrol or mission
Mince meat	see Chapter 2 – British Food
Mind your head	Watch your head
Minge (rhymes with singe)	Woman's genitalia or public hair
Minger (rhymes with singer)	An unpleasant person or thing
Minging	Foul smelling
Mingy	Very small (as in 'She lives in a mingy flat')
Mint	Awesome
Minted	Wealthy
Mithered	Bothered, pestered
Moan	Complain
Mobile phone	Cell phone
Modules	Classes (in college)

Chapter 1 – Everyday Words and Phrases (A to Zed)

UK says:	USA says:
Moggie/moggy	Alley cat (non-pedigree cat similar to 'mutt' for a dog)
Moke	Donkey
Mole grips	Vise grips
Molly-coddled	Looked after (overly looked after)
Mong	Retard (derogatory for someone acting idiotic)
Monged out	High (from drugs or alcohol)
Monobrow	Unibrow
Moose	Ugly woman (derogatory)
Moreish	n/a; tasty food causing one to want more
MOT	n/a; UK Ministry of Transport annual safety and emissions test required for all vehicles over 3 years old
Mot (Irish)	Girlfriend
Motorbike	Motorcycle
Motorway	Highway or freeway
Mothering Sunday	Mother's Day
MP	n/a; Member of Parliament

Chapter 1 – Everyday Words and Phrases (A to Zed)

UK says:	USA says:
Muck about	Goof off, waste time
Muddling	Confusing
Mug	Stupid or gullible person
Mull (Scottish)	Headlands
Multi-story car park	Parking garage
Mum/mummy	Mom/mommy
Munter	Ugly woman
Murder (as in food)	Devour or crave
Muppet	Idiot, dimwit
Mutt's nuts	see 'dog's bollocks'

Chapter 1 – Everyday Words and Phrases (A to Zed)

N

UK says:	USA says:
Naff	Uncool, tacky, cheap, unfashionable
Naff off	Get lost, go away
Nail varnish	Nail polish
Naked flame	Open flame
Nancy boy	Pathetic or weak male; also used for a gay man
Nappies	Diapers
Narked	Annoyed, irritated
National Insurance	Social Security (UK equivalent) withdrawn from wages
Natter away	Chatter away, talkative
Natty	Fashionable, cool
Naughty bits	Naked parts, privates
Nause	Highly irritating person
Navvy	Road or railway construction worker/laborer
Near go	Near miss
Nearside (of a car)	Curbside (left side in the UK)
Ned (Scottish)	Drunken brawling male

Chapter 1 – Everyday Words and Phrases (A to Zed)

UK says:	USA says:
Needn't	Don't need to
Nesh	Wimp
Nethers	Genitals (generic)
New lease of life	New lease on life
Newsagent	News stand
Newsreader	Newscaster
NHS	National Health Service (UK government medical system)
Nicked (1)	Arrested (by the police), busted
Nicked (2)	Stole (as in something was taken); see also 'pinched'
Niggle	Persistent discomfort
Nightdress	Nightgown
Nil	None
Ninny	Foolish and weak person
Nip	Go quickly (as in, 'nip' down to the petrol station)
Nipper	Young boy, kid
Nob	Highbrow, usually someone of nobility
Nonce	Sex offender
Nobble	Sabotage, hinder
Nosh	Food
Nosy parker	Busybody
Note (as in money)	Bill
Nought	Zero (the number)

Handy Guide to British English: Understanding the "English" Language

Chapter 1 – Everyday Words and Phrases (A to Zed)

UK says:	USA says:
Noughties, The	The 2000s decade
Noughts and crosses	Tic-tac-toe
Nous	Shrewdness, good sense
Nowt	Nothing
Number plate	License plate
Numpty (Scotland)	A lovable idiot (endearing term)
Nut	Head butt
Nutter	Crazy person

Chapter 1 – Everyday Words and Phrases (A to Zed)

O

UK says:	USA says:
OAP	Retiree, senior citizen; acronym for Old Age Pensioner
Odds and sods	Odds and ends
Off colour	Pale or ill
Off licence store	Liquor store
Off one's chump	Gone crazy, mad
Off one's own bat	Spontaneously
Off the peg	Off the rack (ready-made instead of made to order)
Off you go	Go ahead, get started
Off your head	Off your rocker, out of your mind
Off your trolley	Mad, crazy
Offal	Butchered animal's internal organs
Offside (of a car)	Streetside; side farthest from the curb (right side in the UK)
Oi	Hey!, exclamation used for getting someone's attention
Oik	Low class or obnoxious person

Chapter 1 – Everyday Words and Phrases (A to Zed)

UK says:	USA says:
Old bean	n/a; friendly greeting to a man
Old Bill	Police
Omnibus	n/a; a series of previously aired episodes on TV or radio re-broadcast together
On holiday	On vacation
On offer	On sale
On tenterhooks	On edge; anxious
On the fiddle	Cheating, swindling
On the piss	Going drinking (with the intention of getting drunk)
One-off	One time occurrence or event such as a sale
One-to-one	Face-to-face, one-on-one
Open day	Open house
Opencast mining	Open pit mining
Ordinary share	Common stock
Orientated	Oriented
Oughtn't	Ought not, shouldn't
Outwith (Scotland)	Outside
Oven glove	Oven mitt
Overtake	Pass (on a highway)
Overtaking lane	Passing lane
Over the moon	Extremely please or excited
Owt	Anything

Chapter 1 - Everyday Words and Phrases (A to Zed)

P

UK says:	USA says:
Paddling pool	Wading pool
Paddy	Rage, fit of temper
Paki	Slang for someone from Pakistan
Pan (Scotland)	Break (as in, don't 'pan' the window)
Pants	Underwear
Paper round	Paper route
Paracetamol	Acetaminophen
Paraffin	Kerosene
Parky	Chilly, cold
Part ex	Trade in (car trade in)
Partner (relationship)	Live-in girlfriend or boyfriend (legal civil partnership in UK)
Pass	I don't know (literally that's what it means...lol)
Pasting	Take a beating, soundly defeated
Pasty	see Chapter 2 - British Food
Pastille	Lozenge
Patience (the game)	Solitaire

Handy Guide to British English: Understanding the "English" Language

Chapter 1 – Everyday Words and Phrases (A to Zed)

UK says:	USA says:
Pavement	Sidewalk
Pavement pizza	Vomit, puke
Pay packet	Pay envelope
Pay and display	n/a; parking system where pay meter dispenses a ticket that must be displayed on vehicle windows
Peanuts	Cheap
Pear-shaped	Belly up, something gone very wrong
Peckish	Hungry
Pedestrian crossing	Crosswalk
Peedy (Scotland)	Small
Peeler (N. Ireland)	Policeman
Peevish	Sullen
Peg	Clothes pin
Pelican crossing	Pedestrian crossing controlled by lights activated by the pedestrian
Pensioner	Retiree
Penultimate	Next to last; penultimate is used much more frequently in the UK than in the US
People mover	Minivan
Pernickety	Persnickety, fastidious
Perspex	Plexiglass
Pervy	Pervert

Chapter 1 – Everyday Words and Phrases (A to Zed)

UK says:	USA says:
Pet hate	Pet peeve
Petrol	Gas, gasoline
Petrol-head	Motorhead; someone with a keen interest in cars
Phiz	Face
Phone box	Phone booth
Phut	Broken, something has stopped working
Physiotherapy	Physical therapy
Pig's ear	Make a mess, muddle
Pikey	Gypsy
Pillar box	Mailbox (for outgoing mail)
Pillar box red	Fire engine red (reference to bright red color)
Pillock	Idiot
Pineapple (Scotland)	Roman Catholic chapel
Pinched	Stole or arrested (see also 'nicked')
Pinny (Pinafore)	Apron

Chapter 1 – Everyday Words and Phrases (A to Zed)

UK says:	USA says:
Pint	Mug of beer or ale, roughly in a pint glass
Pips	Seeds
Pissed	Drunk
Piss off	Get lost
Piss up	Drinking session
Pissing about	Fooling around, goofing off
Pissing it down	Pouring rain, downpour
Pitch	Soccer field, playing field
Plain chocolate	Dark chocolate
Plain flour	All-purpose flour
Plaster board	Drywall
Plastered (Scotland)	Drunk, loaded
Plasters	Band aids
Pleb	Low class (derogatory)
Plectrum	Guitar pick
Plimsolls	Gym shoes, sneakers
Plod	Policeman
Plonk	Cheap wine
Plonker	Inept, foolish, idiot
Plooky (Scotland)	Pimply, spotty
Plough (The Plough)	Big Dipper
Plug point	Electrical outlet
Plug-ugly	Coyote ugly, butt ugly

Chapter 1 – Everyday Words and Phrases (A to Zed)

UK says:	USA says:
Poached	n/a; solicited to take a job with another company
Pocket money	Allowance
Po-faced	Overly serious
Polo neck	Turtle neck
Ponce	Poser
Pong	Foul smell, odorous
Pongo	n/a; soldier from the Royal Naval or RAF
Poof, poove	Footrest, ottoman, hassock
Pop one's clogs	Die; pop off
Popped	Pawned (as in "I popped my class ring for 30 quid")
Poppycock	Nonsense
Porkies	Lies
Porridge	Oatmeal; also refers to time in prison
Portaloo	Portapotty, portajohn
Posh	Uppity; high class
Posho	Upper class person
Positive discrimination	Reverse discrimination
Post	Mail
Postbox	Mailbox
Post code	Zip code
Postal order	Money order
Postal vote	Absentee ballot
Postman, postie	Mailman

Chapter 1 - Everyday Words and Phrases (A to Zed)

UK says:	USA says:
Potty	Silly, loony
Pound shop	Dollar store
Power cut	Power outage
Power point	Electrical outlet
Poxy	Disrepair, in bad condition
Pram (perambulator)	Baby stroller
Prang	Car wreck
Prat	Idiot, incompetent
Prawns	Shrimp
Prefect	Head boy in school
Press-up	Push up
Presenter	TV or radio host
Preventative	Preventive
Prise (to prise open)	Pry
Programme	Program
Proper	Real, genuine ('Manchester United has a proper football team this year')
Prybar	Crowbar
PTO	Please Turn Over (used on government forms)
Pub	Bar (short for public house)

Chapter 1 – Everyday Words and Phrases (A to Zed)

UK says:	USA says:
Pub-crawling	Bar hopping
Pub grub	Bar food
Public school	Private school
Public toilet	Restroom
Public transport	Public transportation
Publican	Landlord (of public housing)
Pudding	Dessert (not actual pudding); see Chapter 2 – British Food
Puff	Fart
Pukka	Excellent, good quality
Pull	Attract sexually, looking for a hook up
Punch-up	Fistfight
Puncture	Flat tire
Punter	John, prostitute's client; customer
Pushchair	Stroller
Put paid to	Put an end to it
Put your oar in	Put your two cents worth in
Pylon	Utility pole

Chapter 1 - Everyday Words and Phrases (A to Zed)

Q

UK says:	USA says:
Quality	Excellent, great (as in, that was a 'quality' film)
Quango	Quasi-autonomous government organization (BBC, Forestry Commission)
Quantity surveyor	Estimator
Quay (pronounced 'key')	Shipping dock
Queer as clockwork orange	Very very odd
Query	Question
Queue	Line (as in waiting in line)
Queue up	Get in line
Quid	buck; slang for one British pound sterling
Quids in	Money ahead (profit or benefit from something)
Quim	Woman's genitals
Quin	Quintuplet
Quine (Scotland)	Young women
Quite	Absolutely! (when used alone)
Quorate	Quorum

Handy Guide to British English: Understanding the "English" Language

Chapter 1 - Everyday Words and Phrases (A to Zed)

R

UK says:	USA says:
Racing car	Race car
Radge (Scotland)	Crazy
Rag-and-bone man	Second hand items dealer
RAF	Royal Air Force
Railway	Railroad
Randy	Horny
Rashers	Cuts of bacon
Rat-arsed	Drunk
Recorded delivery	Certified mail
Reckon	Of an opinion (as in "I reckon she's 35 or so")
Redundant (made redundant)	Laid off
Reel of cotton	Spool of thread
Registration plate	License plate
Remould	Retread (tires)
Removal van	Moving van (for household goods)
Renewal	Replacement
Rent boy	Young male prostitute
Return tickets	Round trip tickets
Reverse charge	Collect call
Reversing lights	Back-up lights
Revising	Studying
Richard the Third	Piece of crap, turd

Chapter 1 – Everyday Words and Phrases (A to Zed)

UK says:	USA says:
Right	Very
Right-angled triangle	Right triangle
Right one	Hellion
Ringburner	Curry food (because of its effect on the bowels)
Ring road	Beltway
Road surface	Pavement, blacktop
Road works	Road construction
Roaster (Scotland)	Fool
Rocket	A severe reprimand
Rodgering	Having sex
Ropey	Iffy, poor quality
Rota	Rotation, schedule of duties; shift
Round the bend	A bit crazy
Roundabout (at a fair)	Carousel, mary-o-round
Roundabout (in a road)	Traffic circle
Rounders	Baseball
Row (rhymes with 'cow')	Argument
Rowing boat	Rowboat
Rozzer	Cop, police officer
Rubber	Eraser

Chapter 1 – Everyday Words and Phrases (A to Zed)

UK says:	USA says:
Rubbish (noun)	Trash, garbage
Rubbish (adjective)	Nonsense; lousy
Rucksack	Knapsack, backpack
Rugger	Rugby
Rumpy pumpy	Hanky panky, sex

Chapter 1 – Everyday Words and Phrases (A to Zed)

S

UK says:	USA says:
Sacked	Fired (from one's job)
Sackcloth	Burlap
Sad	Uncool (similar use as 'naff')
Sailing boat	Sailboat
Saloon (car)	Sedan
Sandpit	Sandlot
Sandwich cake	Layer cake
Sanitary towel	Sanitary napkin
Sarky	Sarcastic
Sat here (as in "I'm sat here waiting for you")	Sitting here; see Chapter 3 – Grammatical Differences
Sat nav	GPS
Sausage fest	Event where men significantly outnumber women (e.g. car show)
Savoury	Non-dessert food
Sawn	Sawed (sawn-off shotgun)
Scally	Hooligan, scallywag
Scarper	Flighty, someone who flees or runs away
Scooby (Scotland)	Clue (as in, "We have no 'scooby' as to we are")
Scouse	n/a; slang for someone from Liverpool
Screw	Prison guard

Chapter 1 – Everyday Words and Phrases (A to Zed)

UK says:	USA says:
Scrote	Scrotum
Scrubber	Tramp, promiscuous woman
Scrum	Rowdy crowd
Scrummy	Delicious
Scrump	n/a; steal from an orchard or garden
Scrumple	Crumple (as in, "I scrumpled up the paper and binned it")
Scrumpy	Strong cider drink (alcoholic)
Scunnurt (Scotland)	Disgusted
Scuppered	Sank (boat or ship)
Secateurs	Pruning shears
Secondary school	High school
Secondment	Temporary assignment
See a man about a dog	Have to go to the bathroom
See the wood for the trees	See the forest for the trees
Self-raising flour	Self-rising flour
Sell-by-date	Expiration date (mainly for perishable food)
Sellotape	Scotch tape
Semi-detached (house)	Duplex
Send-up	Make fun of something or someone, a take-off

Chapter 1 – Everyday Words and Phrases (A to Zed)

UK says:	USA says:
Septic	Yank, American
Serviette	Napkin
Settee	Sofa
Shagging	Having sex
Shambles	Big mess, chaos
Shambolic	Chaotic, disorganized
Shandy	see Chapter 2 – British Food
Shank's pony	On foot, walking
Shan't	Shall not, won't
Share option	Stock option
Shat	Past tense of sh*t
Shattered	Exhausted, extremely tired
Shedload	A lot; large quantity of (variation of "sh*tload")
Shell suit	Track suit
Shilling	n/a; unit of currency prior to the pound
Shire	County (similar to a county in the US)
Shirtlifter	Homosexual, fag (derogatory)

Chapter 1 – Everyday Words and Phrases (A to Zed)

UK says:	USA says:
Shirty	Bad tempered, angry, have an attitude
Shite	Sh*t; minor curse word variation of sh*t
Shitehawk	Someone who is worthless
Shocking (as in "She looks shocking")	Terrible
Shoot the cat	Vomit
Shop	Store
Show home	Model home
Shufflebutt	Restless, fidgety
Shufti	Take a look at something
Sick	Vomit (as in, "I was cleaning up my son's sick")
Sickie	Hooky, sick leave when not actually sick
Silencer (on a car)	Muffler
Silverside	see Chapter 2 – British Food
Single ticket	One-way ticket
Sixes and sevens	Topsy turvy, messed up, gone haywire
Skeleton in the cupboard	Skeleton in the closet
Skelp (Scotland)	Smack or hit someone
Sketch	Skit (as in a comedy skit)
Skew-whiff	Crooked, not straight, askew
Skimmed milk	Skim milk
Skin and blister	One's sister (rhyming slang)

Chapter 1 - Everyday Words and Phrases (A to Zed)

UK says:	USA says:
Skint	Broke (as in having no money)
Skip	Dumpster
Skipping rope	Jump rope
Skirting board	Baseboard
Skive	Play hooky, avoid work
Skiver	Slacker, lazy
Skivvying	n/a; doing menial house work
Skuddy (Scotland)	Naked
Slag	Tart, promiscuous woman; also used for badmouthing someone
Slag heap	n/a; pile of industrial waste
Slagging off	Insulting, denigrating criticism
Slap and tickle	Heavy petting, making out
Slap head	Bald man
Slap up meal	Elegant meal
Slapper	Slut, tramp
Slash	Urinate, pee
Sledge	Sled
Sleeper	Railroad tie
Sleeping partner	Silent partner
Sleeping policeman	Speed bump

Chapter 1 – Everyday Words and Phrases (A to Zed)

UK says:	USA says:
Slip road	Exit ramp (on a highway)
Slippy	Slippery
Sloshed	Drunk
Slowcoach	Slowpoke
Smalls	Underwear
Smarmy	Sleazy 'player', smooth talker with the ladies
Smart casual	Business causal, sharp dressed
Smart jeans	Dressy jeans (not blue jeans)
Smashing	Awesome
SMS	Text message
Snakes and ladders	Chutes and ladders (board game)
Snog	Kiss
Snookered	Between a rock and a hard place, defeated
Soap dodger	Unclean, odorous person
Sod	Moron, bastard
Sod it!	I give up!
Sod off	Piss off

Handy Guide to British English: Understanding the "English" Language

Chapter 1 – Everyday Words and Phrases (A to Zed)

UK says:	USA says:
Sod's Law	Murphy's Law (anything that can go wrong, will go wrong)
Solicitor	Attorney; lawyer (for contracts and personal matters in lower courts)
Sorted	Resolved, problem solved
Soya bean	Soybean
Spanner	Wrench
Spare wheel	Spare tire
Spawny	Lucky
Speed hump	Speed bump
Spend a penny	Go to the bathroom
Spiffing	First rate, excellent
Splashback	Backsplash
Splash out	Spent too much money
Split	Betray, sell out
Split pin	Cotter pin
Spring onion	Green onion
Spod	Nerd or someone socially awkward
Spoilt	Spoiled
Spot on	Just right or absolutely correct
Sprog	Child, offspring
Sprogging	Having a baby

Chapter 1 – Everyday Words and Phrases (A to Zed)

UK says:	USA says:
Squaddle	Non-commissioned soldier, grunt
Squidgy	Soft, spongy, moist
Squiffy	Tipsy, slightly drunk; something gone wrong
Squint (Scotland)	Crooked, not straight
Stabilizers	Training wheels
Stag do	Bachelor party
Stanley knife	Utility knife
Starkers	Naked; stark naked
Starter	Appetizer
State school	Public school
Steady on	Calm down, hold your horses
Steaming	Extremely drunk
Sterling	Awesome; great (can also refer to money as in British Pound Sterling)
Sticky wicket	Sticky situation
Stodgy	Heavy, filling (as in food)
Stock-take	Take inventory
Stone (as in "She looks great having lost a stone")	n/a; measure of weight equal to 14 lbs
Stone the crows	Holy cow! (exclamation)
Stonker	Erection, boner

Handy Guide to British English: Understanding the "English" Language

Chapter 1 – Everyday Words and Phrases (A to Zed)

UK says:	USA says:
Stonking	Something impressive, huge
Stoor (Scotland)	Dust
Storm in the teacup	Tempest in the teapot
Straight away	Right away, immediately
Strawberry creams	Women's breasts
Streamer	Weed whacker
Stroke (/)	Slash (/)
Stroppy	Ill-tempered, sulking
Stuffed	Sexual intercourse
Subway	Tunnel under a road for pedestrians
Suck it and see	Take your chances
Sultanas	Golden raisins
Sump	Oil pan
Sun cream	Sunscreen
Sunday roast	see Chapter 2 – British Food
Surgery	Doctor's office
Surname	Last name
Suspender belt	Garter belt (women's)
Sussed	Figured it out
Swarf	Metal chips
Sweating cobs	Incredibly hot and sweaty
Swede	Rutabaga
Sweep it under the carpet	Sweep it under the rug
Sweets	Candy
Swimming costume	Bathing suit

Chapter 1 - Everyday Words and Phrases (A to Zed)

UK says:	USA says:
Swizz	Something disappointing or a scam
Swotting	Studying hard, cramming

*Handy Guide to British English:
Understanding the "English" Language*

Chapter 1 – Everyday Words and Phrases (A to Zed)

T

UK says:	USA says:
T's & C's	Terms & Conditions (of a contract)
Ta	Thank you
Table tennis	Ping pong
Table a motion	Recommend something, to put it on the table (completely opposite to US usage where to table a motion is to park it); see Chapter 3 – Grammatical Differences
Taff, Taffy	n/a; slang for someone from Wales
Take it with a pinch of salt	Take it with a grain of salt
Takeaway (as in food)	Takeout; carry-out; to go
Taking the biscuit	Takes the cake, can't be out-done
Taking the mickey out of	Making fun of
Taking the piss out of	Making fun of
Takings	Receipts of money
Talent	Sexy young girls
Tally-ho	n/a; used when something has been spotted (originally from foxhunting); similar to 'land-ho'

Chapter 1 – Everyday Words and Phrases (A to Zed)

UK says:	USA says:
Tannoy	PA system
Tap	Faucet
Tap (Scotland)	Borrow (as in, can I 'tap' a fiver off ye?)
Tardis	n/a; phone booth serving as a time machine (from the 'Dr. Who' series); often used to describe a deceivingly large interior space
Tart	Tramp, sexually provocative woman
Tatty	Old-fashioned or worn out
Tea	Dinner
Tea break	Coffee break
Tea towel	Dish towel
Telly	TV; television
Tenner	n/a; 10 pound British note or 10 quid
Term	Semester (in school)
Tetchy	Irritable
That's a sin (Scotland)	What a shame

Chapter 1 – Everyday Words and Phrases (A to Zed)

UK says:	USA says:
Theater	Where plays, ballets, etc. are held (in the UK movies are viewed in cinemas)
Third party insurance	Liability insurance
Throw a spanner in the works	Throw a monkey wrench into it
Tickety-boo	Things are going well
Timescale	Timeframe
Timetable	Schedule
Tick	Check mark
Ticks your boxes	Meets your desires
Ticket tout	Scalper
Ticking over	Idling
Tidy	In reference to an attractive female
Tights	Pantyhose
Till	Cash register, check-out
Timber	Lumber
Tin	Can
Tip	Messy, as in "his room is a tip"
Tipping	Dumping, throwing something away
Tipple	Alcoholic drink, spirits

Chapter 1 – Everyday Words and Phrases (A to Zed)

UK says:	USA says:
Titbit	Tidbit
Titchy	Very small
Tits up	Something gone awry
Tod	n/a; unit of measure equal to 28 lbs of wool
Todger	Penis
Toerag	Scum bag
Toff	Rich or upper class person (derogatory), posh
Toffee apple	Candy apple
Toffee-nosed	Stuck up
Tog	n/a; measure of warmth used for comforters (duvets)
Toll motorway	Toll road, turnpike
Toilet	Bathroom
Tomato sauce	Ketchup
Tonk	Hit hard; also means to be muscular, ripped, buff
Tool	Penis
Top	Shirt
Top drawer	Top notch

Chapter 1 – Everyday Words and Phrases (A to Zed)

UK says:	USA says:
Top up	Top off, add to; one can 'top-up' a drink glass or mobile phone minutes, etc.
Torch	Flashlight
Tosh	Nonsense, baloney
Tosser	Jerk, asshole (see 'wanker')
Touch wood	Knock on wood (superstition)
Tout (ticket tout)	Scalper (of event tickets)
Town centre	Downtown
Trade union	Labor union
Tracky bottoms	Sweatpants
Trading estate	Industrial park
Trainers	Sneakers, tennis shoes
Tram	Street car, cable car
Transport cafe	Truck stop
Traveller	Gypsy or nomadic person
Treacle	Molasses
Trilby	Type of British style hat
Trodden on	Stepped on

Chapter 1 - Everyday Words and Phrases (A to Zed)

UK says:	USA says:
Trolley	Shopping cart, buggy
Trolley dolly	Airline stewardess
Trollop	Tramp, promiscuous woman
Trousers	Pants, slacks
Trump	Fart, toot
Truncheon	Night stick (used by police)
Trunk call	Long-distance call, toll call
Tube	Subway or metro
Turf accountant	Bookie
Turned up	Showed up
Turnover (as in sales)	Revenue
Twelve-bore	Twelve-gauge
Twally (Scotland)	Dumb person
Twee	Overly dainty or quaint, sentimental
Twig	Realize or catch on to something
Twigs and berries	Male genitalia
Twit	Idiot
Twitchy	Nervous

Handy Guide to British English: Understanding the "English" Language

Chapter 1 – Everyday Words and Phrases (A to Zed)

UK says:	USA says:
Two finger salute	Middle finger; vulgar gesture where two fingers in the V shape are pointed at you (thumb facing you)
Two ticks	Two seconds
Two-up two-down	n/a; a house with 2 rooms downstairs and 2 bedrooms upstairs
Twonk	Idiot, fool
Tyre	Tire (of a vehicle)
Tyre lever	Tire iron

Chapter 1 – Everyday Words and Phrases (A to Zed)

U

UK says:	USA says:
Unalike	Unlike
Under-fives	Toddlers, pre-K; loosely refers to children under 5 years old not yet in full time school
Underground	Subway
Undertake	Commence; begin
Uni, university	College
Untoward	Problematic
Unwell	Sick
Up the duff	Pregnant
Up the pole	Crazy, mad
Up the stick	Pregnant
Up sticks	Move, go live elsewhere, pull up stakes
Uphill gardener	Homosexual male

Chapter 1 – Everyday Words and Phrases (A to Zed)

V

UK says:	USA says:
VAT	n/a; acronym for Value Added Tax
Vacuum flask	Thermos bottle
Value for money	Good deal; very common British expression for getting a good deal for your money
Veg	Vegetable
Verge (in a road)	Shoulder
Vest	Tank top; tank shirt
Veterinary surgeon	Veterinary
Video	VCR
Vom	Vomit

Chapter 1 – Everyday Words and Phrases (A to Zed)

W

UK says:	USA says:
WAG	n/a; media term for 'Wives and Girlfriends' of celebrities, especially professional soccer players (footballers)
WC (acronym for water closet)	Bathroom, public restroom
Wagon (on a train)	Car
Waffle on	Ramble on
Wage packet	Paycheck
Waistcoat	Vest (worn with 3-piece suit)
Walking frame	Walker
Wally	Foolish, silly, or inept person
Wangle	Lucky, cleverly manipulative
Wanker	Idiot or someone who masturbates (typically used as a derogatory insult similar to 'a jerk off')
Wanking	Masturbating
Wardrobe	Closet

Handy Guide to British English: Understanding the "English" Language

Chapter 1 - Everyday Words and Phrases (A to Zed)

UK says:	USA says:
Washing	Laundry (waiting to be washed)
Watershed	n/a; the time at night when UK television shows can show nudity and foul language)
Way out	Exit ('way out' is used as exit sign)
Wazzock	Annoying person, idiot
WC	Public bathroom, acronym for 'Water Closet'
Wedding tackles	Man's genitals
Wee	Pee, urinate (as in "I need to take a wee")
Wee (Scotland)	Little, as in a "He was a wee man"
Weegie (Scotland)	n/a; someone from Glasgow
Wellies (short for Wellingtons)	Rain boots, galoshes
Wendy house	Playhouse (for children)
Wheelarch (on a car)	Wheel well

Chapter 1 – Everyday Words and Phrases (A to Zed)

UK says:	USA says:
Wheelie bin	Rolling trash can
Whilst	While
Whinge	Whine, complain, moan about something
Whip-round	Take up a collection (a collection of money from a small group of people for a specific purpose, e.g. a gift for co-worker)
White coffee	Coffee with cream/milk
White spirit	Mineral spirits
White van man	n/a; used to describe an aggressive driver of a delivery or worker's van (typically a white van)
Wholemeal bread	Whole wheat bread
Wicked	Way cool, excellent
Willy	Penis
Willy-waving	Macho (acting overly macho)
Winch (Scotland)	French kiss
Windcheater	Windbreaker
Winds	Farts, as in "he's got the winds"
Windscreen	Windshield

Chapter 1 – Everyday Words and Phrases (A to Zed)

UK says:	USA says:
Wind up	Make fun of
Wing (of a car)	Fender
Winkle	Penis
Wittering on	Muttering, talking to oneself
Wizard	Excellent, way cool
Wizzo	Excellent
Wobbly	Fit of anger or panic, tantrum
Wonga	Money
Wonky	Crooked or askew, not quite right, shaky
Woolly	Vague, confusing
Worktop	Countertop
Wouldn't say boo to a goose	Wouldn't hurt a fly; describes a timid or non-aggressive person
Write-off (a damaged asset)	Totaled, total loss

Chapter 1 – Everyday Words and Phrases (A to Zed)

Y

UK says:	USA says:
Y-fronts	Tightie whities
Yallright	Are you all right?; used as a general greeting predominantly in the north, "Hiya, yallright?"
Yampy	Mad, crazy
Yank	American; Brits' common non-derogatory reference to Americans
Yob	Punk, young hooligan
Yocker (Scotland)	n/a; large stone but not too large to throw
Yomp	n/a; a long walk across rough terrain
Yonks	A long time
Yummy mummy	Attractive, stylish young mother

Chapter 1 – Everyday Words and Phrases (A to Zed)

Z

UK says:	USA says:
Zapper	TV remote control, channel changer
Zebra crossing	Pedestrian crossing
Zed	Z (as in the letter 'Z'); Brits do not say 'zee'
Zimmer frame	Walker
Zip	Zipper
Zonked	Exhausted

Chapter 2 – British Food

UK food:	What is it?
A	
Apple dragon (Wales)	See bakestone (with grated apple added)
Arctic roll	Dessert of vanilla ice cream wrapped in a layer of sponge cake with raspberry jam lining
Atholl brose (Scotland)	A festive beverage made by mixing oatmeal brose, honey, whiskey, and cream
B	
Bacon	English bacon is not the thin strip pork bacon, rather it is thick smoke-cured fried pork loin (back bacon); similar to Canadian bacon
Bakestones (Wales); also known as Welsh cakes	Cakes containing flour, sultanas, raisins, and cinnamon or nutmeg baked on a cast iron griddle or bakestone
Bakewell tart	Baked open pie (no top crust) lined with jam and filled with almond sponge cake with a cherry on top
Bangers	Sausages (English sausage)
Bangers and mash	Sausage and mashed potatoes

Chapter 2 – British Food

UK food:	What is it?
Bannock (Scotland)	Round flat quick bread cut in wedges (wedges sometimes called scones)
Banoffee pie	Dessert pie made of bananas, cream, and toffee
Barmbrack (N. Ireland)	Leavened bread with sultanas and raisins
Bap	Bun or bread roll
Bara brith (Wales)	A rich cake
Barm	Bun
Beans on toast	Baked beans on toast
Bedfordshire clanger	Elongated suet crust dumpling with both sweet (jam or fruit) and savory (meat, potato, vegetables) filling at each end
Beef Wellington	Fillet steak coated with a pate paste and wrapped in pastry
Berwick cockle (Scotland)	Candy mints with red stripes and cockle-like shape
Bickey	Biscuit
Biscuits	Wafers, cookies (not like doughy US biscuits)
Black bun (Scotland)	Large fruit cake wrapped in thick pastry
Black pudding	Blood sausage made from pork blood and oatmeal

Chapter 2 – British Food

UK food:	What is it?
Blancmange	Molded gelatin dessert
Bloater	A whole herring that has been salted, smoked, and cured; served cold (see also 'buckling')
Boxty (N. Ireland)	Pancake serving of grated potato mixed with mashed potato, flour, and buttermilk
Branston pickle	Diced vegetables made into a pickled chutney
Brawn	Head cheese (non-dairy); jellied meat from the head of a calf or pig (see also 'souse')
Bread-and-butter pudding	Traditional dessert of sliced bread and butter with layers of dried fruit
Bree (Scotland)	Soup
Bridie (Scotland)	Meat pastry consisting of minced steak, butter, and beef suet (hard fat)
Brose (Scotland)	An uncooked form of porridge
Brown sauce	Spicy and tangy dark sauce made from a mixture of ketchup and Worcestershire sauce

Chapter 2 – British Food

🇬🇧 UK food:	🇺🇸 What is it?
Bubble and squeak	Traditional English dish made of fried leftover roast vegetables chopped and mixed with mashed potatoes
Buckling	A whole herring that has been salted, smoked, and cured; served hot (see also 'bloater')
Butty	Sandwich
C	
Caboc (Scotland)	Scottish cream cheese
Cake	
Cawl (Wales)	Stew made with bacon, lamb, and vegetables
Chip butty	Fries on a bun (basically a french fry sandwich)
Chippy	A fish and chips shop
Chips	Fries
Christmas pudding	Festive pudding made of suet with dried fruits, dark sugar, and spices
Cider	Alcohol beverage made from apple juice (hard cider)
Clapshot (Scotland)	Traditional dish of turnips mashed together with potatoes and chives, served with haggis, oatcakes, and meat

Chapter 2 – British Food

🇬🇧 UK food:	🇺🇸 What is it?
Clotted cream	Very thick cream that is spread with a knife
Cob	Round loaf of bread
Cock-a-leekie soup (Scotland)	Soup made of leeks and chicken stock, thickened with rice or barley
Cockle (Wales)	An edible, salt water clam often served with breakfast
Colcannon (N. Ireland)	Mashed potatoes with kale or cabbage
Comet	Ice cream cone
Corn	Wheat (England); oats (Scotland)
Corn flour	Corn starch
Cornish pasty	A crust pastry pie made of meat and vegetables – usually beef, potato, swede, and onion (originated in Cornwall)
Cottage loaf	Bread in the shape of a figure eight from two balls of dough baked together with the smaller ball on top
Cottage pie	Essentially same as Shepard's pie; meat pie with a top layer of crusted mashed potatoes
Crisps	Potato chips

Handy Guide to British English:
Understanding the "English" Language

Chapter 2 - British Food

UK food:	What is it?
Cream tea	Traditional snack consisting of tea, scones, with clotted cream and strawberry jam
Crowdie (Scotland)	Type of Scottish cream cheese
Crubeens (N. Ireland)	Boiled pigs' feet
Crumpet	English muffin
Cullen skink (Scotland)	Thick soup of smoked haddock, potatoes, and onions
Cumberland sausage	Variety of sausage traditionally made in a very long curl of pork meat, spices, herbs, and pepper
Currant	Type of raisan
Custard	Sweet creamy sauce served with various desserts
D	
Digestives	Sweetish wholemeal biscuits (cookies) with digestive benefits usually eaten with tea or coffee
Demerera sugar	Brown sugar
E	
Eton mess	Dessert of mixed whipped cream, pieces of meringue, and strawberries

Chapter 2 – British Food

UK food:	What is it?
Egg banjo	Runny fried egg sandwich
Eggy bread	French toast
F	
Faggots (Wales)	Meatballs made from pig or lamb's liver, onions, and oats
Fairy cake	Cupcake
Fillet (pronounced phonetically as 'FILL-it')	Fillet; boneless piece of meat or fish
Fish and chips	Deep fried fish (usually battered cod or haddock) and fries
Fish fingers	Fish sticks
Fish pie	Puff pastry filled with white fish (cod or haddock) in cream sauce
Flapjack	Granola bar
Flies graveyard	Sweet pastry squares filled with raisins or currants that resemble dead flies
Flummery	Soft mousse dessert
Fry up	Another name for 'full English breakfast'
Full English breakfast	Traditionally includes poached or fried eggs, fried or grilled tomatoes, fried mushrooms, toast, sausages, baked beans, fried potatoes or potato

Chapter 2 – British Food

UK food:	What is it?
	cake, black pudding, and tea
G	
Gammon	Ham
Gentleman's Relish	Anchovy paste typically spread on toast
Gherkin	Pickle
Ginger wine	Wine made from fermented ground ginger root and raisins
Glamorgan sausage (Wales)	Traditional Welsh vegetarian sausage made of cheese, leeks, and breadcrumbs
H	
Haggis (Scotland)	Sheep's heart, liver, and lungs minced with onion, oatmeal, and spices encased in the animal's stomach (or sausage casing)
J	
Jacket potato	Baked potato
Jam butty	Jam sandwich
Jam roly-poly	Pudding made of jam or fruit rolled in a pastry and steamed or baked
Jam split (Wales)	Welsh cake cut horizontally with jam added in sandwich fashion
Jammie dodgers	Popular shortbread biscuit

Chapter 2 – British Food

UK food:	What is it?
	with raspberry jam filling
K	
Kippers	Breakfast fish; a whole small herring that has been butterfly sliced, salted, pickled, and smoked
Knickerbocker Glory	Ice cream sundae with fruit served in a tall glass
L	
Laver bread (Wales)	Traditional Welsh delicacy made from seaweed and oatmeal
Leeks	Very similar to onions
Leek soup (Wales)	Soup made with diced potatoes, sautéed leeks, chicken broth, and cream
Lincolnshire sausage	Variety of sausage made of pork meat, spices, and the herb sage
Lobscows (Wales)	Stew made of steak, potatoes, and vegetables
Lorne sausage	See 'square sausage'
M	
Manchester tart	A shortcrust pastry shell spread with raspberry jam, custard filling, with coconut flakes and cherry on top

Chapter 2 – British Food

UK food:	What is it?
Marmite	Brand name of a sticky, dark brown savory food paste spread on toast or biscuits
Marrow	Squash (the vegetable)
Mince meat or minced meat	Ground beef
Mince and tatties (Scotland)	Popular dish of minced beef (usually cheaper cut) and mashed potatoes
Mince pie	
Mint sauce	Finely chopped spearmints leaves soaked in vinegar; often used on roast lamb
Mulled wine	Wine made with red wine and spices served hot; typically a winter beverage
Mushy peas	Mashed garden peas like mashed potatoes
N	
Neeps (Scotland)	Another name for swede (rutabaga)
P	
Panackelty	Casserole dish made of corned beef and root vegetables (potatoes, onions)
Parkin	Spicy cake with oatmeal and ginger

Chapter 2 - British Food

UK food:	What is it?
Partan bree (Scotland)	Crab soup consisting of crab, rice, stock, milk or cream
Pasties	Pies made using a single piece of pastry to wrap around the filling
Pease pudding or pease porridge	Savory pudding with the consistency of hummus made with boiled split peas and spices
Pickled walnuts	Whole-shelled walnuts pickled in vinegar
Pies	Usually refers to savory pies made of crust pastry with various meat and vegetable fillings
Pig's trotters	Cooked pig feet (also called 'pettitoes')
Pilchards	Large sardines
Pint (as in "Give me a pint")	Beer or ale (a pint of ale)
Ploughman's lunch	A cold meal consisting of cheese, chutney, and bread
Pork cracking	Pork rinds
Pork pie	Crust pastry filled with chopped pork and pork jelly
Porridge	Oatmeal
Pub food; pub grub	An assortment of ales, savory pies, fish and chips, etc. usually prepared in the pub

Chapter 2 – British Food

UK food:	What is it?
Pudding	Primarily refers to any type of dessert (see also 'savoury pudding')
R	
Rarebit (Wales)	Melted cheese on toast
Rashers	Slices of back bacon
Rollmops	Pickled herring fillets wrapped cylindrically around a savory filling
Rumbledethumps (Scotland)	Mashed potatoes with cabbage and onion
Runner beans	Green beans
Rusk	Dry, hard biscuit (generally for babies when teething)
S	
Sandwich cake	Layer cake
Sarnie	Sandwich
Savoury pudding	Soft suet casing made with savory ingredients in a cylindrical shape with indented middle for gravy or white sauce
Scones	Single serving of baked quick bread made of wheat, barley, or oatmeal

Chapter 2 – British Food

UK food:	What is it?
Scotch woodcock	Traditional dish of creamy scrambled eggs on toast that has been spread with anchovy paste (Gentleman's Relish)
Shandy	Beer with lemonade
Silverside	Rump roast
Simnel cake	Rich fruit cake covered with icing and decorations eaten during Lent and/or Easter
Singing hinny (Scotland)	Round griddle cake or scone; see also 'bannock'
Skirlie (Scotland)	Breakfast dish made from oatmeal fried with fat, onions, and seasonings
Skits and kidneys (N. Ireland)	Stew made from pork meat, which includes the kidneys
Soldiers	Finger-sized slices of toast
Souse	Head cheese (brawn) pickled with vinegar
Spag bol	Spaghetti bolognese
Spoom	A frothy sorbet typically served in a tall glass
Spotted dick	A popular sponge pudding made with raisins resembling 'spots', commonly topped with custard or cream
Squab pie	Savory pastry crust pie made with lamb and apple filling

Chapter 2 – British Food

UK food:	What is it?
Square sausage (Scotland)	Breakfast sausage made of ground beef and rusk; see also 'Lorne sausage'
Stargazy pie	Famous Cornwall dish where the heads of fish stick out through the pie crust as if they were 'stargazing'
Steak and ale pie	A pastry crust pie made with steak and beef gravy with onions and ale added to the filling
Steak and kidney pie	Traditional savory pie primarily made with a mixture of diced beef and kidney (often lamb or pork), fried onion, and brown gravy in a crust pastry
Steak and kidney pudding	Diced beef and kidney (lamb or pork) and gravy encased in a suet pastry
Stilton	Type of English cheese with two varieties, blue and white containing distinct 'veins'
Stottie cake or stotty	Heavy dough bread made in circular shape with indented middle

Chapter 2 – British Food

UK food:	What is it?
Stovies (Scotland)	Potato dish made with left-over vegetables and minced or roast beef
Sultanas	Golden raisins
Sunday roast	Tradition Sunday meal with roasted meat, various sides or potatoes and vegetables, Yorkshire pudding, and gravy
Swede	Rutabaga
T	
Table sauces	Mustard, ketchup, brown sauce, etc.
Tablet (Scotland)	Traditional hard candy that resembles fudge
Tatties (Scotland)	Mashed potatoes
Tatty ash	Dish of potatoes and corned beef
Tayberry (Scotland)	Cross between a blackberry and red raspberry
Tea	Dinner (evening meal)
Tea cake	Traditional toasted and buttered sweet bun with dried fruit
Tipsy cake	Sponge cake saturated with wine or whiskey

Chapter 2 – British Food

UK food:	What is it?
Toad in the hole	Traditional British dish of sausages in Yorkshire pudding served with onion gravy with vegetables
Treacle	Molasses
Trifle	Cold sponge cake covered with fruit and layers of cream, jelly, and custard
Tripe	Edible stomach offal of various farm animals
Turmut, tates, and mate	Turnip, potatoes, and meat typically used in pasty fillings
U	
Ulster fry (N. Ireland)	Irish breakfast with potato bread but without white pudding
V	
Veg	Any type of vegetable; veggies; "Tonight we are having a meat and veg for tea."
Victoria sponge	A 2-layer sponge cake filled with jam and buttercream
W	
Welsh cakes	see 'Bakestones'

Chapter 2 – British Food

UK food:	What is it?
Whitebait	Sardine-like silvery-white young fish (like herring) eaten in numbers
White coffee	Coffee with cream
White pudding (Scotland and N. Ireland)	Oatmeal pudding made of pork meat, fat, bread, and oatmeal into a large sausage
Wholemeal bread	Whole wheat bread
Whortleberry pie	Basically a blueberry pie
Y	
Yorkshire pudding	Traditional batter pudding made of eggs, flour, and milk usually served with gravy and is a staple of a Sunday roast (see 'Sunday roast')

Chapter 3 – Grammatical Differences

There are many grammatical differences between British English and American English that will seem a bit odd when you read it or hear it in conversation. This chapter provides a short synopsis of some of the more common differences.

Verb Tense Confusion

You will hear and read confusing verb tense, that at first you will think is improper grammar; however it has become the English way (although not necessarily considered proper English). A past tense verb is often used for a present tense action. For example, "I'm <u>sat</u> here waiting on you" where 'sat' is used incorrectly for the present action. See the table of examples below.

UK says:	US says:
I'm <u>sat</u> here on the settee.	I'm <u>sitting</u> here on the sofa.
We were <u>sat</u> in the front row of the football match.	We were <u>seated</u> in the front row of the soccer game.
I'm <u>lay</u> here warm and cozy under the duvet.	I'm <u>laying</u> here warm and cozy under the comforter.
I'm <u>stood</u> here waiting for you to collect me.	I'm <u>standing</u> here waiting for you to pick me up.

Chapter 2 – British Food

UK food:	What is it?
Whitebait	Sardine-like silvery-white young fish (like herring) eaten in numbers
White coffee	Coffee with cream
White pudding (Scotland and N. Ireland)	Oatmeal pudding made of pork meat, fat, bread, and oatmeal into a large sausage
Wholemeal bread	Whole wheat bread
Whortleberry pie	Basically a blueberry pie
Y	
Yorkshire pudding	Traditional batter pudding made of eggs, flour, and milk usually served with gravy and is a staple of a Sunday roast (see 'Sunday roast')

Chapter 3 – Grammatical Differences

There are many grammatical differences between British English and American English that will seem a bit odd when you read it or hear it in conversation. This chapter provides a short synopsis of some of the more common differences.

Verb Tense Confusion

You will hear and read confusing verb tense, that at first you will think is improper grammar; however it has become the English way (although not necessarily considered proper English). A past tense verb is often used for a present tense action. For example, "I'm <u>sat</u> here waiting on you" where 'sat' is used incorrectly for the present action. See the table of examples below.

UK says:	US says:
I'm <u>sat</u> here on the settee.	I'm <u>sitting</u> here on the sofa.
We were <u>sat</u> in the front row of the football match.	We were <u>seated</u> in the front row of the soccer game.
I'm <u>lay</u> here warm and cozy under the duvet.	I'm <u>laying</u> here warm and cozy under the comforter.
I'm <u>stood</u> here waiting for you to collect me.	I'm <u>standing</u> here waiting for you to pick me up.

Chapter 3 – Grammatical Differences

See what I did there? I also threw in a few other British English words and phrases in those examples.

Additionally, in British English plural verbs are often used with collective nouns where singular verbs would be used in the US. See the examples below.

UK says:	US says:
The family have gone on holiday.	The family has gone on vacation.
Manchester United have won another match.	Manchester United has won another match.
Tesco are having a big sale.	Tesco is having a big sale.
The whole family were at the chapel.	The whole family was at the chapel.
The home team were lucky to have won.	The home team was lucky to have won.
The jury have reached a verdict.	The jury has reached a verdict.
When Parliament make a decision...	When Parliament makes a decision...
BBC News have acquired new information...	BBC News has acquired new information...

Chapter 3 – Grammatical Differences

Self-Reference

You often will hear British people refer to themselves in the plural, as 'we' or 'us'. Additionally, British people frequently use 'me' for self-possessive reference instead of 'my'. In northern England, 'me' will also be heard as a redundant auxiliary in reference to self. See the table below for examples.

UK says:	US says:
Give <u>us</u> a kiss.	Give <u>me</u> a kiss.
Give <u>us</u> a bell five minutes before you want <u>us</u> to collect you.	Give <u>me</u> a call five minutes before you want <u>me</u> to pick you up.
<u>We</u> want you to visit again soon.	I want you to visit again soon.
I can't find <u>me</u> shoes.	I can't find <u>my</u> shoes.
Top up <u>me</u> ale, mate.	Refill <u>my</u> beer, pal.
I have to wee, <u>me</u>.	I have to pee.
I'm hungry, me.	I'm hungry.

Chapter 3 – Grammatical Differences

Plurality

There are many British words that do not change from singular to plural. Again, this is not necessarily proper English but is very common.

Word	UK says:
Accommodation	We still don't have adequate holiday <u>accommodation</u> for our family. *American English would use the plural 'accommodation<u>s</u>'.*
Stone (as in measure of weight)	Nigel looks fit after having lost two <u>stone</u>. *American English would use the plural 'stone<u>s</u>'.*
Pound (as in currency)	Tea for two cost us 45 <u>pound</u>. *American English would use the plural 'pound<u>s</u>'.*
Sport	Liam is quite athletic and enjoys <u>sport</u>. *American English would use the plural 'sport<u>s</u>'.*
Wine	I prefer red <u>wine</u> to white. *American English might use the plural 'wines'.*

Chapter 3 - Grammatical Differences

Past Tense (-ed replaced by -t)

The past tense of some verbs in British English that you would expect to end in -ed are modified with the irregular use of -t instead. Some examples are listed in the table below.

UK says:	US says:
Burnt	Burned
Dreamt	Dreamed
Knelt	Kneeled
Leant	Leaned
Leapt	Leaped
Learnt	Learned
Misspelt	Misspelled
Smelt	Smelled
Skint	Skinned
Spelt	Spelled
Spilt	Spilled
Spoilt	Spoiled

Other Grammatical Differences

Table a Motion

Tabling motions in formal meetings have completely opposite meanings between the US and UK. To table

Chapter 3 – Grammatical Differences

a motion in the UK is to open an agenda item for discussion; whereas in the US, to table a motion is to remove or suspend an item from discussion. Interestingly, this difference was documented by Winston Churchill where the opposite meaning of the word *table* caused confusion and misunderstanding during a critical meeting of the Allied Forces.

The use of 'at' instead of 'the':

British English noticeably omits the use of the when referencing institutions such as hospitals or universities. See examples below.

UK says:	US says:
Eleanor's brother works at hospital.	Eleanor's brother works at the hospital.
Ian was injured and taken to hospital.	Ian was injured and taken to the hospital.
I'm off to visit me mum in hospital.	I'm off to visit my mom in the hospital.
Colin studies engineering at university.	Colin studies engineering at the university.
Sarah has been at university for two years.	Sarah has been at the university for two years.

Chapter 3 – Grammatical Differences

The use of 'do', 'needn't', and 'shall':

UK says:	US says:
Q: Are you going into town today? A: I might <u>do</u>.	Q: Are you going into town today? A: I might.
Q: Is she going to see a barrister? A: She should <u>do</u>.	Q: Is she going to see an attorney? A: She should.
Q: Did Alistair like the film? A: He must have <u>done</u>, he saw it twice.	Q: Did Alistair like the film? A: He must have, he saw it twice.
Nigel <u>needn't</u> call a taxi.	Nigel doesn't need to call a taxi.
I <u>needn't</u> go to market today.	I don't need to go to the market today.
<u>Shall</u> we invite Emily to come along?	Should we invite Emily to come along?
I <u>shall</u> visit me mum later.	I will visit my mom later.

Other Grammatical Differences:

UK says:	US says:
Monday <u>to</u> Friday	Monday <u>through</u> Friday
My dog is <u>on heat</u>.	My dog is <u>in heat</u>.

Chapter 3 – Grammatical Differences

UK says:	US says:
I have enrolled <u>on</u> a chemistry class.	I am enrolled <u>in</u> a chemistry class.
Chat <u>to</u> you later.	Chat <u>with</u> you later.
The chip shop is <u>opposite to</u> the church.	The chip shop is <u>opposite of</u> the church.
This pie tastes <u>different to</u> before.	This pie taste <u>different than</u> before.
Me mate has a <u>drugs problem</u>.	My friend has a <u>drug problem</u>.
I live <u>near to</u> the football pitch.	I live <u>near</u> the soccer field.
<u>Apart from</u> the swearing, it was a good film.	<u>Aside from</u> the swearing, it was a good movie.
Liam stepped <u>off</u> the train.	Liam stepped <u>off of</u> the train.
To register one must <u>fill in</u> the form.	To register you must <u>fill out</u> the form.
The word 'river' comes <u>before the name</u>, as in the River Thames.	The word 'river' comes <u>after the name</u>, as in the Mississippi River.
My son is <u>in</u> the football team.	My son is <u>on</u> the soccer team.
The rugby match was <u>rained off</u>.	The rugby match was <u>rained out</u>.
The price of petrol was <u>extortionate</u>!	The price of gas was <u>outrageous</u>!
I had to <u>fork out</u> 50 quid for a parking ticket.	I had to <u>fork over</u> 50 bucks for a parking ticket.
Walk <u>towards</u> the light.	Walk <u>toward</u> the light.

Handy Guide to British English:
Understanding the "English" Language

Chapter 3 – Grammatical Differences

UK says:	US says:
Look <u>upwards</u> to the sky.	Look <u>upward</u> to the sky.
Nigel is a <u>cricketer</u>.	Nigel is a <u>cricket</u> player.
Hesham is a <u>footballer</u>.	Hesham is a football player.
Child abuse is wrong, <u>full stop</u>!	Child abuse is wrong, <u>period</u>!
Abigail <u>read</u> engineering at Oxford.	Abigail <u>majored in</u> engineering at Oxford.
Next Tuesday I <u>sit</u> the final exam.	Next Tuesday I will <u>take</u> the final exam.
Times are tough and my cousin's shop <u>went into administration</u>.	Times are tough and my cousin's shop <u>went into bankruptcy</u>.
Chelsea won the match <u>two-nil</u> (meaning 2-0).	Chelsea won the match <u>two-zip</u> (2-0)
My US visa application was <u>refused</u>.	My US visa application was <u>denied</u>.
<u>Pound sign</u> is £ (currency)	<u>Pound sign</u> is # (number sign)
Happy Christmas!	Merry Christmas!
Date formatting is always day/month/year; example May 5th, 2015 is written as 07/05/2015 or 07-May-2015	05/07/2015 or May-05-2015
I bought sweets for <u>80p</u> (pence).	I bought candy for <u>80 cents</u>. (you would not hear '80c' in the US)
I'll meet you at <u>half nine</u> (9:30).	I'll meet you at 9:30.

Chapter 3 – Grammatical Differences

UK says:	US says:
I'll meet you at <u>quarter to</u> seven (6:45).	I'll meet you at a quarter til (or <u>quarter of</u>) seven.
See you <u>a week on Friday</u>.	See you <u>Friday after next</u>.
<u>Mind</u> your head.	<u>Watch</u> your head.
Mr, Mrs, Dr, St, Dr (no periods are used)	Mr., Mrs, Dr., St., Dr.
I'll meet you at <u>quarter past</u> two. (British usually say 'past' the hour, whereas US say 'after' the hour)	I'll meet you at a <u>quarter after</u> two.
I have already <u>eaten</u>.	I already <u>ate</u>.
<u>I've got to</u> go the loo.	<u>I got to</u> go to the bathroom. (often shortened to "I gotta go to the bathroom"); Brits generally do not say 'gotta'

Handy Guide to British English:
Understanding the "English" Language

Chapter 4 – Pronunciation and Spelling

Pronunciation

Many words are spelled the same in the US and UK, however they may be pronounced very differently. Here are some of the more common words, listed as phonetically pronounced. Note that the emphasized syllable is shown in upper case letters. Where there is equal emphasis on more than one syllable, each will be capitalized (for example, the word 'missile' in the UK is pronounced MISS-ILE with equal emphasis on both syllables, whereas in America emphasis is only on the first syllable MISS-ull).

Word	UK says:	USA says:
Address	uh-DRESS	ADD-ress
Adult	ADD-ult	uh-DULT
Advertisement	ad-VERT-iss-ment	ad-ver-TIZE-ment
Aluminium (aluminum)	al-yoo-MIN-i-um	a-LOO-min-um
Ancillary	an-SILL-uh-ree	AN-sill-ar-ee
Anthony	AN-ton-ee	AN-thon-ee
Apparatus	ap-ar-ATE-us	ap-er-AT-us
Apricot	APE-ri-cot	AP-ri-cot
Ask	OSK (rhymes with 'mosque')	ASK

Chapter 4 – Pronunciation and Spelling

Word	UK says:	USA says:
Banana	ba-NAH-nah	ba-NAN-uh
Baton	BAT-on	buh-TAHN
Beta	BEE-ta	BAY-ta
Bidet	BEE-day	bi-DAY
Brochure	BRO-shuh	bro-SHURE
Buffet	BOO-fay	buh-FAY
Buoy	BOY	BOO-ee
Café	KA-fay	ka-FAY
Chagrin	SHAG-rin	sha-GRIN
Charade	sha-RAHD	sha-RADE
Chauffer	SHO-fah	sho-FER
Clever	KLEV-uh	KLEV-er
Cliché	CLEE-shay	cli-SHAY
Comrade	COM-rod	COM-rad
Contribute	CON-tri-byoot	con-TRIB-yoot
Cremate	cri-MATE	CREE-mate
Crystalline	kris-til-INE	KRIS-til-een
Debris	DAY-bree	de-BREE
Debut	DAY-byoo	day-BYOO
Defence (defense)	de-FENCE	DEE-fence
Director	die-REK-tuh	di-REK-ter
Docile	DOSS-ILE	DOSS-ull
Dynasty	DIN-is-tee	DINE-as-tee
Either	EYE-ther	EE-ther

Handy Guide to British English:
Understanding the "English" Language

Chapter 4 – Pronunciation and Spelling

Word	UK says:	USA says:
Enquiry (inquiry)	in-KWIE-ree	IN-kwer-ee
Fillet	FILL-it	fill-AY
Fragile	FRA-JILE	FRA-jull
Garage	GA-rej	ga-ROJ
Garden	GAH-den	GAR-den
Glacier	GLASS-ee-er	GLAY-see-er
H (the letter)	HAYCH	AYCH
Hurricane	HER-i-cun	her-i-CANE
Jaguar	JAG-you-ah	JAG-wahr
Laboratory	la-BOR-a-tree	LAB-rah-tor-ee
Leisure	LEH-zhuh	LEE-zher
Liaison	lee-AY-zen	lee-AY-zahn
Library	LIE-bree	LIE-breh-ree
Lieutenant	LEF-ten-ant	LOO-ten-ant
Lord	LUWD	LORD
Malaysia	ma-LAY-see-uh	ma-LAY-zhah
Mandatory	man-DATE-o-ree	MAN-da-tor-ee
Margarine	mar-jar-EEN	MAR-jar-in
Mascara	ma-SKAH-rah	mas-KA-ruh
Mayonnaise	may-o-NAZE	MAY-o-naze
Military	MILL-i-tree	MILL-i-ter-ee
Missile	MISS-ILE	MISS-ull
Mobile	MO-BILE	MO-bull
Monarch	MON-ahk	MON-ark
Moustache	moo-STASH	MUS-tash

Chapter 4 – Pronunciation and Spelling

Word	UK says:	USA says:
Neither	NIE-thuh	NEE-ther
New	NYOO	NOO
Party	PAH-tee	PAR-dee
Pastel	PASS-tel	pass-TELL
Patent	PAY-tent	PAT-ent
Patriot	PAT-ree-ot	PAY-tree-ot
Philistine	FILL-i-STINE	FILL-i-steen
Potato	pa-TAH-toe	poe-TATE-oh
Premier	preh-ME-air	pri-MEER
Primer	PRIM-er	PRIME-er
Process	PRO-sess	PRAH-sess
Project	PRO-ject	PRAH-ject
Research	ri-SURCH	REE-surch
Resources	ri-ZORS-es	REE-sorss-es
Route	ROOT	ROUT (although some Americans say ROOT)
Sachet	SASH-ay	sash-AY
Salon	SAL-on	sa-LON
Sanctuary	SANK-choo-ree	SANK-choo-air-ee
Says	SAZE	SEZ
Scarf	SKAHF	SKARF
Scenario	se-NAHR-ee-oh	se-NARE-ee-oh
Schedule	SHED-yool	SKED-yool
Semester	SIM-ist-er	suh-MESS-ter
Smart	SMAHT	SMART

Chapter 4 – Pronunciation and Spelling

Word	UK says:	USA says:
Soprano	suh-PRAH-no	suh-PRAN-oh
Serpentine	SERP-in-tine	SERP-in-teen
Status	STATE-us	STAT-us
Strawberry	STRAW-bree	STRAW-ber-ee
Stupid	STYOO-pid	STOO-pid
Tomato	toe-MAH-toe	toe-MATE-oh
Tower	TOW-uh	TOW-er
Tuesday	TYOOZ-day	TOOZ-day
Tuna	TYOO-nah	TOON-uh
Tunisia	too-NEE-see-ah	too-NEE-zhah
Turbine	TUR-BINE	TUR-ben
Vase	VAHZ	VAYS
Vaccine	VAX-een	vak-SEEN
Vitamin	VIT-a-min	VITE-a-min
Yard	YAHD	YARD
Z (the letter)	ZED	ZEE
Zebra	ZEB-rah	ZEE-brah

Chapter 4 – Pronunciation and Spelling

Spelling

Many words with the same meaning are spelled differently between the US and UK. If you ever plan to live and/or work in the UK, you will need to adjust all your spell check settings to 'UK English or British English'. In fact as I write this book, my spell checker is freaking out at all the words I've listed in the UK column of the table below. ☺

UK spelling:	USA spelling:
Accessorise	Accessorize
Accoutrements	Accouterments
Aeon	Eon
Aerogramme	Aerogram
Aeroplane	Airplane
Aerofoil	Airfoil
Ageing	Aging
Almanack	Almanac
Amphitheatre	Amphitheater
Anaemic	Anemic
Anaesthetist	Anesthetist
Analogue	Analog
Analyse	Analyze
Appal	Appall
Appetiser	Appetizer
Armour	Armor
Artefact	Artifact

Handy Guide to British English:
Understanding the "English" Language

Chapter 4 – Pronunciation and Spelling

UK spelling:	USA spelling:
Aluminium (pronounced al-yoo-MIN-i-um)	Aluminum
Anaemic	Anemic
Appal	Appall
Archaeology	Archeology
Arguement	Argument
Authorise	Authorize
Axe	Ax
B.Sc. or BSc (Bachelor of Science)	B.S. or BS
Bannister	Banister
Banque	Bank
Baulk	Balk
Behaviour	Behavior
Behove	Behoove
Bevvy	Bevy
Biassed	Biased
Bogeyman	Boogeyman
Breathalyse	Breathalyze
Burnt	Burned
Caesarean	Cesarean
Calibre	Caliber
Calliper	Caliper
Callisthenics	Calisthenics
Cancelled, cancelling	Canceled, cancelling
Candour	Candor

Chapter 4 – Pronunciation and Spelling

UK spelling:	USA spelling:
Carburettor	Carburetor
Carolling	Caroling
Catalogue	Catalog
Centigramme	Centigram
Centimetre	Centimeter
Centre	Center
Centrefold	Centerfold
Channelled	Channeled
Cheque	Check
Chequer	Checker
Chilli	Chili
Civilisation	Civilization
Clamour	Clamor
Colour	Color
Colourful	Colorful
Connexion	Connection
Cosy	Cozy
Councillor	Councilor
Counsellor	Counselor
Criticise	Criticize
Cruellest	Cruelest
Cypher	Cipher
Cystallise	Crystallize
Defence	Defense
Demeanour	Demeanor
Dialled, dialling	Dialed, dialing

Chapter 4 - Pronunciation and Spelling

UK spelling:	USA spelling:
Dialogue	Dialog
Diarrhoea	Diarrhea
Digitise	Digitize
Disc	Disk
Discolour	Discolor
Distil	Distill
Doughnut	Donut
Draught	Draft
Draughtsman	Draftsman
Dreamt	Dreamed
Duelling	Dueling
Economise	Economize
Edoema	Edema
Encyclopaedia	Encyclopedia
Endeavour	Endeavor
Enrol	Enroll
Enthral	Enthrall
Enquiry	Inquiry
Epilogue	Epilog
Equalled	Equaled
Faecal	Fecal
Fantasise	Fantasize
Favour	Favor
Favourite	Favorite
Fuelled, fuelling	Fueled, fueling
Fibre	Fiber

Chapter 4 – Pronunciation and Spelling

UK spelling:	USA spelling:
Carburettor	Carburetor
Carolling	Caroling
Catalogue	Catalog
Centigramme	Centigram
Centimetre	Centimeter
Centre	Center
Centrefold	Centerfold
Channelled	Channeled
Cheque	Check
Chequer	Checker
Chilli	Chili
Civilisation	Civilization
Clamour	Clamor
Colour	Color
Colourful	Colorful
Connexion	Connection
Cosy	Cozy
Councillor	Councilor
Counsellor	Counselor
Criticise	Criticize
Cruellest	Cruelest
Cypher	Cipher
Cystallise	Crystallize
Defence	Defense
Demeanour	Demeanor
Dialled, dialling	Dialed, dialing

Chapter 4 – Pronunciation and Spelling

UK spelling:	USA spelling:
Dialogue	Dialog
Diarrhoea	Diarrhea
Digitise	Digitize
Disc	Disk
Discolour	Discolor
Distil	Distill
Doughnut	Donut
Draught	Draft
Draughtsman	Draftsman
Dreamt	Dreamed
Duelling	Dueling
Economise	Economize
Edoema	Edema
Encyclopaedia	Encyclopedia
Endeavour	Endeavor
Enrol	Enroll
Enthral	Enthrall
Enquiry	Inquiry
Epilogue	Epilog
Equalled	Equaled
Faecal	Fecal
Fantasise	Fantasize
Favour	Favor
Favourite	Favorite
Fuelled, fuelling	Fueled, fueling
Fibre	Fiber

Chapter 4 - Pronunciation and Spelling

UK spelling:	USA spelling:
Fibreglass	Fiberglass
Flautist	Flutist
Flavour	Flavor
Foetal	Fetal
Foetus, foetuses	Fetus, fetuses
Fulfil, fulfils	Fulfill, fulfills
Funnelled	Funneled
Furore	Furor
Gaol (old English spelling)	Jail
Gaolbird (old English)	Jailbird
Gaolbreak (old English)	Jailbreak
Gaoler (old English)	Jailer
Gipsy	Gypsy
Glamour	Glamor
Glueing	Gluing
Gramme	Gram
Grey	Gray
Grovelled	Groveled
Groyne	Groin
Gruelling	Grueling
Gryphon	Griffin
Gybe	Jibe
Gynaecology	Gynecology
Haemaglobin	Hemoglobin
Haemaphilia	Hemaphilia
Haemorrhage	Hemorrhage

Chapter 4 - Pronunciation and Spelling

UK spelling:	USA spelling:
Harbour	Harbor
Homoeopathic	Homeopathic
Honour	Honor
Honourable	Honorable
Humour	Humor
Idolise	Idolize
Inflexion	Inflection
Initialled	Initialed
Instal	Install
Instalment	Installment
Instil	Instill
Ionise	Ionize
Itemise	Itemize
Jewellery	Jewelry
Jewelled	Jeweled
Judgement	Judgment
Kerb (roadway edge)	Curb
Kilogramme	Kilogram
Kilometre	Kilometer
Labelled, labelling	Labeled, labeling
Labour	Labor
Labourers	Laborers
Lacklustre	Lackluster
Leant	Leaned
Leapt	Leaped
Learnt	Learned

Chapter 4 – Pronunciation and Spelling

UK spelling:	USA spelling:
Leukaemia	Leukemia
Levelled	Leveled
Libelled	Libeled
Licence (noun)	License
Likeable	Likable
Liquidise	Liquidize
Liquorice	Licorice
Litre	Liter
Louvre	Louver
Lustre	Luster
M.Sc. or MSc (Master of Science	M.S. or MS
Manoeuvre	Maneuver
Marvellous	Marvelous
Matt	Matte
Meagre	Meager
Memorise	Memorize
Metre	Meter
Midiaeval	Medieval
Misspelt	Misspelled
Mobilise	Mobilize
Modelled	Modeled
Monologue	Monolog
Mould	Mold
Moults	Molts
Moustache	Mustache

Chapter 4 – Pronunciation and Spelling

UK spelling:	USA spelling:
Mum	Mom
Neighbour	Neighbor
Neighbourhood	Neighborhood
Normalise	Normalize
Odour	Odor
Oesophagus	Esophagus
Oestrogen	Estrogen
Offence	Offense
Omelette	Omelet
Orientated	Oriented
Organisation	Organization
Orthopaedic	Orthopedic
Oxidise	Oxidize
Paediatrician	Pediatrician
Paedophile	Pedophile
Palaeontology	Paleontology
Panelled	Paneled
Paralyse	Paralyze
Parlour	Parlor
Pedalling	Pedaling
Pencilled	Penciled
Per cent	Percent
Phial	Vial
Philtre	Filter
Phoney	Phony
Plough	Plow

Chapter 4 – Pronunciation and Spelling

UK spelling:	USA spelling:
Ploughman	Plowman
Pouffe	Pouf
Practise	Practice
Preventative	Preventive
Prioritise	Prioritize
Prise	Pry
Practise	Practice
Pretence	Pretense
Primaeval	Primeval
Prioritise	Prioritize
Programme	Program
Prologue	Prolog
Pyjamas	Pajamas
Pzazz	Pizazz
Quarrelled	Quarreled
Rancour	Rancor
Ravelled	Raveled
Realise	Realize
Reflexion	Reflection
Refuelling	Refueling
Rigour	Rigor
Rivalled	Rivaled
Rumour	Rumor
Sabre	Saber
Sanitise	Sanitize
Saviour	Savior

Chapter 4 - Pronunciation and Spelling

UK spelling:	USA spelling:
Savoury	Savory
Sawn	Sawed
Sceptical	Skeptical
Scepticism	Skepticism
Sceptre	Scepter
Sheikh	Sheik
Shovelled	Shoveled
Skilful	Skillful
Skinned	Skint
Smoulder	Smolder
Snorkelling	Snorkeling
Snowplough	Snowplow
Sombre	Somber
Speciality	Specialty
Spectre	Specter
Spiralled	Spiraled
Spilt	Spilled
Splendour	Splendor
Spoilt	Spoiled
Standardise	Standardize
Storey	Story
Storeys	Stories
Sulphate	Sulfate
Sulphides	Sulfides
Sulphur	Sulfur
Syphon	Siphon

Chapter 4 – Pronunciation and Spelling

UK spelling:	USA spelling:
Ploughman	Plowman
Pouffe	Pouf
Practise	Practice
Preventative	Preventive
Prioritise	Prioritize
Prise	Pry
Practise	Practice
Pretence	Pretense
Primaeval	Primeval
Prioritise	Prioritize
Programme	Program
Prologue	Prolog
Pyjamas	Pajamas
Pzazz	Pizazz
Quarrelled	Quarreled
Rancour	Rancor
Ravelled	Raveled
Realise	Realize
Reflexion	Reflection
Refuelling	Refueling
Rigour	Rigor
Rivalled	Rivaled
Rumour	Rumor
Sabre	Saber
Sanitise	Sanitize
Saviour	Savior

Handy Guide to British English:
Understanding the "English" Language

Chapter 4 - Pronunciation and Spelling

UK spelling:	USA spelling:
Savoury	Savory
Sawn	Sawed
Sceptical	Skeptical
Scepticism	Skepticism
Sceptre	Scepter
Sheikh	Sheik
Shovelled	Shoveled
Skilful	Skillful
Skinned	Skint
Smoulder	Smolder
Snorkelling	Snorkeling
Snowplough	Snowplow
Sombre	Somber
Speciality	Specialty
Spectre	Specter
Spiralled	Spiraled
Spilt	Spilled
Splendour	Splendor
Spoilt	Spoiled
Standardise	Standardize
Storey	Story
Storeys	Stories
Sulphate	Sulfate
Sulphides	Sulfides
Sulphur	Sulfur
Syphon	Siphon

Chapter 4 – Pronunciation and Spelling

UK spelling:	USA spelling:
Technicolour	Technicolor
Theatre	Theater
Titbit	Tidbit
Tonne	Ton
Traveller, travelling	Traveler, traveling
Toxaemia	Toxemia
Tranquillise	Tranquilize
Travelogue	Travelog
Tumour	Tumor
Tyres (on a car)	Tires
Unalike	Unlike
Unequalled	Unequaled
Unsavoury	Unsavory
Urbanisation	Urbanization
Utilise	Utilize
Valour	Valor
Vapour	Vapor
Vice (as in the tool)	Vise
Vigour	Vigor
Vocalise	Vocalize
Waggon	Wagon
Weaselled	Weaseled
Whilst	While
Whisky	Whiskey
Wilful	Willful
Woollen	Woolen

Chapter 4 - Pronunciation and Spelling

UK spelling:	USA spelling:
Worshipped	Worshiped
Yoghurt	Yogurt
Zed	Z

Chapter 5 - Other Handy Information

What Comprises the UK?

The United Kingdom (UK) is comprised of 4 countries - England, Wales, Scotland, and Northern Ireland. The UK is generally considered part of Europe.

What is Great Britain?

Great Britain is the <u>island</u> that comprises England, Wales, and Scotland. Northern Ireland is located just west of Great Britain on a separate island and is the only UK country that physically borders another country, the Republic of Ireland.

Chapter 5 – Other Handy Information

So then Who is British?

This is the tricky part. The term 'British' typically refers to anyone living in any of the UK countries, however most British people identify with the UK country in which they live. For example, people from Wales are Welsh, people from Scotland are Scottish, people from Northern Ireland are Irish, and people from England are English; however most people who live in England will simply say they are British.

What are the Capitals of the UK Countries?

England – London
Wales – Cardiff
Scotland – Edinburgh (pronounced ED-in-bur-oh)
Northern Ireland – Belfast

What about the Isle of Man and the Channel Islands?

The Isle of Man and the Channel Islands of Guernsey and Jersey are self-governing sovereignties that are <u>not part of the UK</u>; however they are considered Crown dependencies where the British government is responsible for military defense and international representation.

Chapter 5 - Other Handy Information

What about the British Commonwealth?

The UK has a relationship with the Commonwealth of Nations (formerly the British Commonwealth), which consists of 53 member states or countries that were once part of the British Empire, but today are <u>not part of the UK</u>. Queen Elizabeth II is officially the 'Head of the Commonwealth', which is purely symbolic.

Commonwealth Member Nation	Location
Antigua and Barbuda	Atlantic Ocean
Australia	Southern Hemisphere
Bahamas	Atlantic Ocean
Bangladesh	Asia
Barbados	Atlantic Ocean
Belize	Central America (Yucatan Peninsula)
Botswana	Southern Africa
Brunei	Sub-Asia
Cameroon	Central Africa
Canada	North America
Cyprus	Mediterranean Sea
Dominica	Atlantic Ocean (Lesser Antilles)
Fiji	South Pacific Ocean
Ghana	West Africa
Grenada	Atlantic Ocean (Lesser Antilles)

Chapter 5 - Other Handy Information

Commonwealth Member Nation	Location
Guyana	South America
India	Asia
Jamaica	Caribbean Sea
Kenya	Central Africa
Kiribati	Pacific Ocean
Lesotho	Southern Africa
Malawi	Southern Africa
Malaysia	Sub-Asia
Maldives	Indian Ocean
Malta	Mediterranean Sea
Mauritius	Indian Ocean
Mozambique	Southern Africa
Namibia	Southern Africa
Nauru	South Pacific Ocean (Micronesia)
New Zealand	South Pacific Ocean
Nigeria	West Africa
Pakistan	Asia
Papua New Guinea	South Pacific Ocean (Melanesia)
Rwanda	Central Africa
St. Kitts and Nevis	Caribbean Sea (Leeward Islands)
Saint Lucia	Caribbean Sea (Lesser Antilles)
Saint Vincent and the Grenadines	Caribbean Sea (Lesser Antilles)
Samoa	South Pacific Ocean
Seychelles	Indian Ocean (Africa)

Chapter 5 - Other Handy Information

Commonwealth Member Nation	Location
Sierra Leone	West Africa
Singapore	Sub-Asia
Solomon Islands	South Pacific Ocean (Melanesia)
South Africa	Southern Africa
Sri Lanka	Indian Ocean
Swaziland	Southern Africa
Tanzania (including Zanzibar)	Central Africa
Tonga	South Pacific Ocean (Polynesia)
Trinidad and Tobago	Caribbean Sea
Tuvalu	South Pacific Ocean (Polynesia)
Uganda	Central Africa
United Kingdom	North Atlantic Ocean (Europe)
Vanuatu	South Pacific Ocean (Melanesia)
Zambia	Southern Africa

UK Overseas Territories

The UK has direct jurisdiction and sovereignty of 14 overseas territories; however <u>they do not make up part of the UK</u>:

UK Territory	Capital	Location
Akrotiri and Dhekelia	Episkopi Cantonment	Cyprus (military annexes)

Chapter 5 – Other Handy Information

UK Territory	Capital	Location
Anguilla	The Valley	Caribbean Sea (Lesser Antilles)
Bermuda	Hamilton	North Atlantic Ocean
British Antarctica Territory	Rothera	Antarctica (research and support)
British Indian Ocean Territory	Diego Garcia	Indian Ocean (Chago Archipelago)
British Virgin Islands	Road Town	Caribbean Sea
Cayman Islands	George Town	Caribbean Sea (Greater Antilles)
Falkland Islands	Stanley	South Atlantic Ocean
Gibraltar	Gibraltar	Iberian Peninsula (southern tip of Spain)
Montserrat	Brades	Caribbean (Lesser Antilles)
Pitcairn Islands	Adamstown	South Pacific Ocean (best known for where the *Bounty* mutineers settled)
Saint Helena, Ascension, Tristan de Cunha	Jamestown	South Atlantic Ocean
South Georgia and South Sandwich Islands	King Edward Point	South Atlantic Ocean
Turks and Caicos Islands	Cockburn Town	Atlantic Ocean (north of Haiti; Lucayan Archipelago)

Chapter 5 – Other Handy Information

Currency

All countries of the UK use the British Pound Sterling (GBP) as currency. The symbol for GBP or pound is £. 100 pence = 1 pound.

The 'pound' is often referred to as 'quid' for slang, similar to 'bucks' being used as slang for US dollars (USD). Pence are often referred to by simply saying "p", as in 'the sweets cost 80p'. As an example, the amount £4.30 would be quoted as "4 pound, 30p".

Interestingly, although Northern Ireland and the Republic of Ireland are neighbors located on the same island, the UK country of Northern uses the British Pound Sterling (GBP) while the Republic of Ireland uses the Euro as its currency.

Paper currency in the UK is referred to as 'notes', such as a 10 pound note, whereas in the US paper currency is known as 'bills' or 10 dollar bill. Save yourself some embarrassment; do not say "10 pound bill" while in the UK.

Chapter 5 – Other Handy Information

Driving

It is important to note that the British *motorway* system is designed to drive on the <u>left side</u> of the road. Traffic circles or *roundabouts* take traffic in the clockwise direction, opposite from the US. Many of the UK territories and Commonwealth countries also drive on the left. Please consider this if you plan to rent a car (*car hire*) in the UK or Commonwealth countries.

Typically, you can rent a car (*car hire*) anywhere in the UK with a valid US driver's license.

Keep Calm and Carry On

In 1939, the British government issued the 'Keep Calm and Carry On' motivational poster intended to raise the morale of the British people in anticipation of World War II enemy air strikes. In recent years, the 'Keep Calm...' theme has become a staple of UK pop culture. You will see signs, posters, t-shirts, and other merchandise <u>everywhere</u> with some variation of the 'Keep Calm...' theme; such as 'Keep Calm and Drink

Chapter 5 – Other Handy Information

Tea', 'Keep Calm and Avoid Zombies', 'Keep Calm and Eat Chocolate', etc.

Other Handy Tips

- Date formatting is always day/month/year; for example May 5th, 2015 is written as 07/05/2015 or 07-May-2015. Americans could easily confuse 07/05/2015 as July 5th, 2015. It is very important to get this right when scheduling transportation or determining event dates.

- When taking the train, you will need to know your 'platform' which is simply the track number for your train.

- A 'fortnight' is a commonly used term in the UK for a period of two weeks. A 'fortnight Saturday' means the Saturday two-weeks from now.

- A mixed bag of metrics and imperial units of measure are used in the UK. Mileage is still used for distance on road signs instead of kilometers (as used in the rest of Europe).

Chapter 5 – Other Handy Information

Personal height may be quoted in centimeters (*centimetres*) or inches. Food will generally be measured in grams and gasoline (*petrol*) will be shown in *litres*.

- Personal weight is usually quoted in stone (one stone = 14 lbs), whereas kilograms (*kilogrammes*) are typically used for other weights and are often quoted as 'kg'. Easy conversion; 1 kg = 2.2 lbs. A Brit will typically <u>not</u> know their weight in pounds (lbs) or kg. Instead, they will quote their weight as, for example, "I weigh 10 stone, 8 pounds'" meaning 148 lbs (or 67 kg in most of the world).

- UK temperature is usually quoted in Celsius; however Fahrenheit is still widely used. As a quick rule of thumb, to convert a Celsius quote to Fahrenheit for temperatures above freezing (0°C), simply double it and add 32. Example; 13°C would be roughly 58°F, calculated as (2x13) + 32 = 58. The actual conversion for 13°C is 55.4°F. So you can see that the rule of thumb is not exact, but close enough.

Chapter 5 – Other Handy Information

- As previously mentioned, paper currency in the UK is referred to as a 'note', such as a 10 pound note; whereas in the US paper currency is known as a 'bill' or 10 dollar bill. Save yourself some embarrassment; do not say "10 pound bill" while in the UK.

- Most merchants in the UK prefer 'chip-and-pin' credit and debit cards. Usually merchants will take your 'swipe' credit or debit cards at the checkout (*till*), however often times the clerk/cashier will have to call for assistance because 'swipe' cards are not commonly used.

- Computer keyboards are different between the two countries and will take a bit of getting used to. Most notably, the left-most Shift key on US keyboards is a double-wide key, whereas in the UK it is a single key to the far left causing the user to stretch the left finger farther left to Shift. This will feel a bit awkward at first.

Chapter 5 – Other Handy Information

- Bring a raincoat or umbrella (*brolly*) with you at all times because it is going to rain. I repeat; it is going to rain.

- Also bring a sweater (*jumper*) during summer because even summer nights can get quite cool.

- Electrical outlets in the UK are the 230/240V, 3-prong style. Travelers from the US and Europe will need a converter.

- The UK international dialing code is +44. To call a UK number from outside the UK you must dial 00-44-then the remaining number.

Chapter 5 – Other Handy Information

Safety Tips

- The national emergency number throughout the UK is **999** (similar to the 911 emergency number in the US).

- You must <u>look to the RIGHT</u> at all pedestrian crossings (*zebra crossings*) in the UK. This is difficult to get used to as your natural tendency will be to look left. This handy tip is very important for your personal safety – Look to your right before crossing!!

Sources

This project was a labor (*labour*) of love. Nina and I have had a blast putting this book together! There is no specific reference or source that needs citation herein. Much of the content for this book came from conversations with family and friends (*mates*), interaction at work, or watching TV (*telly*) or movies (*films*) where different words and phrases were used, as well as from our many travels within the UK or Commonwealth countries that included many different cuisines. We have also done countless hours of research via information freely available on the internet. Having a British wife was the most effective source for this non-British author. We have both learned (*learnt*) a great deal about our versions of the English language during this project and had many laughs in the process.

We sincerely hope you find this handy guide both fun and informative, and we solicit your feedback. Please feel free to contact us at handyguidetobritishenglish@gmail.com to offer information that we might use for the next edition.

Keep calm and carry on!